WILTSHIRE MISCELLANY

FOR MY MOTHER — with my love

Wiltshire Miscellany

By J. A. Leete

A Moonraker

MELKSHAM
COLIN VENTON
WHITE HORSE LIBRARY

ISBN 0 85475 127 0 (cloth)

United States of America,
The British Book Centre Inc.,
153 East 78th Street,
New York,
N.Y., 10021, U.S.A.

Set 10 on 12 point Intertype Imperial,
and printed in Great Britain
at the Press of the Publisher,
The Uffington Press,
Melksham, Wiltshire.

CONTENTS

ILLUSTRATIONS

All grouped in the centre of the book.

AUTHOR'S FOREWORD

In writing this book my aim has been to create a true Miscellany of Wiltshire, and embody those things which I like and which have interested or amused me.

It will be obvious that I am proud of my County and I hope this work does justice to it, but it is not meant as a guide. I offer my readers a Moonraker's Anthology with the hope that it will give them as much pleasure to read as it has given me to write.

J. A. LEETE.

AN INTRODUCTION TO MY COUNTY

WILTSHIRE is a strange, compelling county, in some minds, its outline resembling a stretched out tobacco leaf or animal pelt held against the sunlight, its corners touching Hampshire, Berkshire, Oxfordshire, Somerset, Dorset, Gloucestershire and Avon. So hemmed in, it might easily be overlooked or forgotten, but, from time immemorial, it has stood proud and strong with that unerring tenacity that brings its children back and back again to its grassy boundaries.

Looking at the bare sketch map of my county, I could believe, appropriately enough, that it was a rough drawing of a primitive man. The squat face, blunted nose and short neck so characteristic of our forebears are there, and perhaps significant of those who roamed its desolation in far gone times.

In its past lies its strength and its future. Some — ignorant of its charm — might think that, possessing no sea, it was bare and rude and wild, but therein, for me, lies its charm. I could gaze and gaze at its free, uncluttered spaces—those rolling downs which stretch, seemingly, to eternity, and turn, refreshed and renewed. Its very timelessness is a reassurance and to know that one can leave its boundaries, travel the world over to return and see Stonehenge still standing proudly is wonder indeed.

Though there is no sea lapping its shores there is a richer harvest — no golden rolling sands cluttered with people, but a glorious tidal wave of green that stretches, rages and swells as any temperamental sea with a quality unmatched.

Our ancestors walked the selfsame downs, their sheep grazed its lush pastures and drank from those dewponds early men learnt to fashion from the chalk soil with secrets handed down from one family to another until no longer needed.

Like a great, chalk giant, the county stretches and relaxes as a cat across the broad width of England, settling itself into position in the same, high born manner. It is territory hard won for, generations ago, its land was war tossed, but now its peaceful tranquillity flows as a melody.

The great Salisbury Plain in the south mellows into the woodland and forests in a tumble of tiny streams and fringes of forest into Dorset and Hampshire, stretching its tentacles as a hand whose fingers are reluctant to surrender their hold.

There is another, some say more beautiful, downland stretch near Marlborough giving a superb panoramic view on all sides as one travels from Devizes, the rolling hills making a superb backcloth to any journey. However often one gazes at them, one always feels that behind them lies the end of the world, or, in some moods, that they dip to the tossing sea. The Marlborough Downs span a great, wide stretch of broad green land and it is fitting that they break their spell with the magic of that unique place, Savernake Forest. This romantic, brooding woodland that weaves and stretches for miles in an endless sea of trees, is still the property of a subject, just as it was in the days when King John hunted there. Some say it is still haunted and the great oaks have a tale to tell. It was here that Henry VIIIth hunted, courted Jane Seymour of Wulfhall, deep in its heart, and took her to be his favourite Queen. The harsh cry of a hunting horn can often be heard by those who listen on a dark night when fear stalks the unwary.

Across the downs, which, in themselves can be found much of England's history, can be seen the same tracks walked by prehistoric men a thousand years ago on their way to the coast or to the fairs with their sheep and cattle. The tracks they made are as timeless as the monoliths and barrows with which they are covered—like a great tracery, weaving its way through life. What a tale they unfold!

Wiltshire is rich in antiquity. Some counties may boast a barrow or two, but Wiltshire can match this with countless burial grounds and chambers in long forgotten fields and secret places. The greatest treasures, so long a part of the landscape as to be almost unnoticed by the locals (though secretly they are justly proud of their heritage) are the great mysteries of Avebury and Stonehenge. It is said the latter was unremarked until James I visited it in 1620 when he asked Inigo Jones, busily engaged in rebuilding work and not specially interested, to discover their secret. No one has penetrated the hidden truths though many, high and low, have come to wonder and marvel at those unique treasures which have no equal in the world.

If you seek buildings, Wiltshire has a rich harvest to offer. Salisbury is one of the most beautiful Cathedrals in the country set in a City that is rich in the past, yet throbbing with the present. There are stately homes, little towns and villages, each with their own special charm, a canal with locks and bridges designed by Brunel — the whole stepping out from the pages of time.

MOONRAKER LEGEND

For more than two hundred years, Wiltshire folk have been nicknamed "Moonrakers" and, though other places claim the distinction of being the originators of the legend, Bishops Cannings is the recognised one.

Outsiders or "furriners" as we call them, thought Wiltshiremen were rustics, in smocks, sucking straws, little realising what perspicacity lay behind that, to the ignorant, dull exterior. Born of a rugged county, the natives had long learned to come to terms with their environment, to make the best of a situation and, if possible, turn it to their own advantage.

In the nineteenth century, smuggling was rife and packloads of contraband were brought along the ancient pathways from Dorset into Wiltshire. The Excisemen were ever vigilant.

Legend says that, one night, just as some men from Bishops Cannings were unloading their precious cargo, the warning came that the Excisemen were coming. Quickly, the men pushed the barrels into the pond, and, foiled, the Excisemen left. The Wiltshiremen took up their long rakes and began trying to rescue their booty, when, full of suspicion, the Excisemen returned.

Luckily, there was a full moon, and when questioned as to why they were raking in the pond, the men replied that they were raking up the cheese, pointing to the moon's reflection in the water. Laughing, the Excisemen returned to Devizes, shaking their heads over the stupidity of the moonrakers. But it was the Wiltshiremen who had the last laugh when they recovered, and enjoyed, their contraband, and, to this day, are proud to be called "Moonrakers", for it proves that, far from being stupid as the Excisemen imagined, they possessed a great deal of sense and what might be called native cunning. For, like the fox, the Wiltshireman can take care of himself and it is a clever man who gets the better of him.

ADAM'S GRAVE

In a county with such antiquity as Wiltshire, it is natural that there should be an Adam's Grave, though even Moonrakers would not claim the occupant was "The Adam".

This Neolithic longbarrow lies near Alton Barnes and is a chambered tomb similar to those at East and West Kennett. It stands some one hundred and thirty feet long and twenty feet high, and ditches on either side which are still twenty feet wide and three feet deep. Traces of a sarsen stone burial chamber are visible at the east end, and when opened in 1860 by John Thurnam it was found to contain parts of three or four skeletons and a leaf-shaped arrow head.

In AD 592 the barrow was known as Wodnesbeorg when Ceol and Caewlin fought beside it.

AN ADVERTISEMENT OF 1827

The following advertisement appeared in Wiltshire in 1827.

Melksham

Mrs Cochrane continues to educate young ladies in English, Geography, History, plain and ornamental needlework, French, Writing, Arithmetic, Drawing, Dancing and Music with the assistance of the Most Approved Masters.

AIRMAN'S CROSS

At the junction of the busy A 3440 and A 360 roads on Salisbury Plain stands a small, simple cross which is a memorial to an early aviator.

It commemorates Captain Loraine and Staff Sergeant Wilson who died in the first fatal air crash on Salisbury Plain, in July 1912.

ST. ALDHELM

One of the County's most famous clerics, he is said to have discovered the quarries at Hazelbury, and it is to him that the building of St Lawrence Church at Bradford on Avon is attributed.

The story is that he was riding near Box one day when he threw down his glove, and told his men to dig there and they should find treasure. They did so, found the quarry and built the church.

AMBRE'S FORTIFIED PLACE

Known originally as Ambre's fortified place, Amesbury is an ancient town, first noted in the ninth century and bequeathed by Alfred to his youngest son.

Clustering on the edge of the great Salisbury Plain, it lies within striking distance of Stonehenge and is much a place of legend, for here stood the "holy house of Almesbury" in which Queen Guinevere took refuge.

There was once a Saxon nunnery and the great church is the ancient Abbey church. It was remade by the Normans who changed it into the Cathedral of the Valley, and it contains fragments of a Saxon wheel in a glass case, a Norman font on a carved base which has stood there for five hundred years and some fifteenth and sixteenth century roods. In the aisle roof is a carving showing Henry VIIIth as a cherub! The Normans did their work well and the whole is impressive and dignified.

Amesbury Abbey today is a Palladian mansion on the site of the original abbey and where Gay wrote his *Beggar's Opera.*

Once Amesbury shared a distinction with Borseley in Shropshire of making the best pipes in England. The trade waned, but specimens of the pipes, with their distinctive gauntlet marking can be found in museums and collections.

ARCHAEOLOGY

The word archaeological is synonymous with Wiltshire, there being so many archaeological monuments to be found that it would require a special book to write about them.

No English county has greater wealth of archaeological treasure than Wiltshire and none can equal the great monuments of Avebury and Stonehenge which are perhaps its most famous.

The great chalk mass of the soil attracted settlers from earliest times and the sarsen stone provided a perfect material for the countless chambered tombs, stone circles and hill forts so common in this area.

Of the two thousand and more round barrows recognised, a great many still remain with the best preserved groups are Winterbourne Stoke (sixty-eight here) or Normanton where the forty are said to be among the best in Britain.

Each age is represented from the Bronze Age barrows just mentioned to the Iron Age with the many hill forts still recognisable — Figsbury and Yarnbury and others — but Roman works are few.

Though the great monuments like Avebury and Stonehenge have been carefully nurtured and preserved, it is unfortunate that a great many other sites have, probably through ignorance or thoughtlessness, been ploughed up. However, there are still many remaining for those who wish to seek them out and perhaps learn more of our forebears.

LADY BLANCHE ARUNDELL

During the Civil War, Wardour Castle was staunchly defended against the Roundheads by Lady Blanche Arundell and twenty-five men. The garrison held out for five days before resistance was useless and the gallant lady signed terms for an honourable surrender — which the enemy promptly broke.

During the gallant defence, Lady Arundell and other ladies of the house loaded up the small arms for the soldiers, and her ghost is said to haunt the castle grounds at night, moving towards the lake.

The last Arundell of Wardour died in 1944, and deaths in this family were presaged by the appearance of white owls.

JOHN AUBREY

One of Wiltshire's most famous sons, he was born near Chippenham in 1626 and educated at Malmesbury and Trinity College, Oxford. Though he entered the Middle Temple in 1646, he was never called to the Bar, and in 1652 succeeded to his estates in Wiltshire.

He was immensely interested in his county and was the earliest topographical historian of Wiltshire, being especially remembered as an antiquary and folklorist.

Aubrey had many love affairs one of which led to his temporary arrest after a lawsuit, but he did find peace in the home of Lady Long of Draycote House where he "dwelt in quietness and comfort, diligently pursuing his favourite studies."

On a journey from London to Draycote, he was taken ill at Oxford where he died in 1697, and buried in the church of St Mary Magdalene.

Perhaps best remembered for his *Brief Lives*, his *Natural History of Wiltshire* makes fascinating reading.

AVEBURY

The standing stones of Avebury represent one of the largest henge monuments left today, and it is considered older than Stonehenge from where some of the famous Circle stones came.

One of the most important early Bronze Age Temples in Europe, it is world known, and the earliest structures date back to 2,500 BC, in the late Neolithic Age.

The village must be unique for the greater part lies within the Circle and attractive cottages, some thatched, were originally constructed from stones removed from the Circle for the purpose.

There are some ninety-eight Sarsen stones, some weighing over thirty tons, in a great circle, of which two quadrants have been restored. The whole encloses some twenty-eight acres and is about thirteen hundred feet in diameter.

Avebury is a strange place—seemingly a continuing surprise, for the stones stretch out along the sides of the main road, looking as natural as trees, and it is sometimes hard to realise it was once considered the greatest Megalithic monument in the world.

In contrast to this great and fascinating antiquity, the old church with its Anglo - Saxon origins and Norman additions, seems almost modern, though its unusual font is a Saxon treasure.

When the museum, which is just north of the church, was built, workmen discovered an interesting collection of pottery and relics.

The body, it was thought, of a tailor or barber, was found buried under one of the stones, who evidently died in the fourteenth century. A leather pouch with him contained silver pennies of the reign of Edward I and there was also a pair of scissors.

Avebury is another of Wiltshire's very, very old treasures, but, somehow, for me, at any rate, this does not seem one of the unhappy ones. Maybe, it is because of the present structure, with the stones spaced out, that makes it so different. There are many who feel it is haunted, but, whereas the ghosts of Stonehenge have a tragic connection, those of Avebury seem to have left happiness behind.

WILLIAM AYSCOUGH

In the fifteenth century, William Ayscough was Bishop of Salisbury and Confessor to Henry VI. He was a man of some importance and influence.

Jack Cade's Rebellion and the ensuing violence forced him to escape from the tumult at Salisbury and he fled to Edington Monastery where he took refuge in the time-honoured way of seeking sanctuary.

On the 29th June 1450, he was dragged from the High Altar during Mass in the Church and brutally murdered in the fields outside. His mutilated body was interred at Edington, and, in 1540, a Chapel and hermitage stood at the site of his murder.

THE B HOUSE GHOST

The M Dormitory in B House at Marlborough College is said to be haunted. Writing as an Old Marlburian in 1888, one boy recalls that the "gentleman occupies his time in throwing himself out of the window, apparently to remind spectators of the crowning folly of an ill-spent life."

He is said to have been scarce of late years so perhaps he has given up the struggle!

In C House — the old Castle Inn, there is the ghost of a man who "merely looks at you which is very weird and shadowy." It is said to be seen mostly by those who play truant from evening Chapel — so maybe he is a clergyman looking reprovingly on those who sin. Some think the ghost of a young woman wringing her hands in silence or pointing an accusing finger might be more impressive!

BEAR HOTEL, DEVIZES

For nearly four centuries, this fine old inn has dominated the scene in Devizes Market Place, its first landlord, John Sawter, taking over in 1599.

An old coaching inn, its heyday was in the eighteenth century when it was a favourite stopping place for travellers journeying to Bath. Perhaps its most famous landlord was Thomas Lawrence, father of the famous portrait painter of the same name.

He was the thoughtful landlord who set up 12 foot high posts, half a mile apart, across Salisbury Plain for the guidance of travellers. On one side they bore the letter D for Devizes and S for Salisbury on the other.

A large stone bear, leaning nonchalantly on the porch of the hotel was originally resting on a column in the middle of the Market Place.

Once, one of the windows bore a pathetic message.

John Blome, merchant, on his way from London to Bath and Bristol for execution, February, 1760.

I wonder what crime he perpetrated to deserve this fate?

JOHN BENT

This brave man was one of Wiltshire's martyrs. A tailor in the village of Urchfont, he strongly denied the doctrine of transubstantiation.

In 1523, he was condemned to death and suffered the terrible agonies of a public burning in Devizes Market Place.

THE BIBURY CLUB

Founded in 1681 at Bibury in Gloucestershire, the Bibury Club is thought to be the oldest racing club in the world. In the reign of Charles II the headquarters of this racing club was like another Newmarket Heath and visited by the Sovereign on three occasions.

In 1681 the Newmarket Spring Meeting was transferred to Bibury. The Club moved to Stockbridge and later to Salisbury after it had held its meetings at Bibury and Burford for over one hundred and fifty years.

Salisbury Races, held on the Race Plain, are among the oldest in England, the first race being recorded was in 1585, and attended by — among others — the Earls of Cumberland, Warwick, Pembroke and Essex.

Henry, Earl of Pembroke (1570—1601) is said to have instituted the Salisbury Races and given a golden bell, worth £50, to be competed for annually. At the first meeting, it was competed for and won by the Earl of Cumberland.

In the seventeenth century, there were two courses at Salisbury one of fourteen miles in length which began at Whitesheet Hill and ended at Harnham Hill, and another which was four miles long. A shorter course began at the edge of the north down of the farm of Broad Chalk and ended at Hare Warren, belonging to the Earl of Pembroke.

A horse called Peacock belonging to Sir Thomas Thynne ran the four mile course in five minutes.

Racing flourished and the Mayor and Corporation of Salisbury provided money for plate as prizes as did George II.

It was in 1899 that Bibury Club moved to Salisbury, and for many years only members of the Club were eligible to participate.

Salisbury Race Course has known many famous visitors including Queen Elizabeth I who is said to have enjoyed a day's racing three months before Drake sailed to defeat the Armada in 1588. Among the famous horses who have run this course are Mill Reef who ran his first race there, Brigadier Gerard his second and Tudor Minstrel with Sir Gordon Richards in the saddle.

THE BIRDS OF SALISBURY

Curious large birds resembling albatrosses with dazzling white wings have a strange and sinister connection with Salisbury. Superstition claims that they are seen, hovering over the Bishop's Palace, their wings still as they fly, whenever a Bishop is dying.

In 1885, Miss Moberley saw them rise from the ground in the Palace Garden, their wings silent and unmoving, just before the death of her father — the Bishop. And, in 1911, they were seen again by Miss Edith Olivier when returning to the City, and later she heard the Bishop had died suddenly.

Some explanations of this curious happening have been that the birds are really angels, which would perhaps explain their motionless flight and dazzling appearance.

A BOATING TRAGEDY

St John's Churchyard in Devizes has a strange monument in the form of an obelisk, some fifteen feet high.

It was erected in 1751 to commemorate the death by drowning of five persons who, on a Sunday in that year, were drowned in Drews Pond, through their unskilful management of a cooler, in which, for lack of a boat, they had ventured to take the water.

The epitath reads (though the engraving is worn with age):

In Memory of the sudden and awful end of Robert Merrit and Susannah his wife Eliz. Tiley her sister Martha Carter, and Josiah Derham, who were all Drowned in the flower of their Youth in a Pond near this Town called Drews on Sunday Evening the 30*th June* 1751 *and are buried together underneath.*

On the base of the obelisk is engraved a warning: *Remember the Sabbath day, to keep it holy.*

"BOOTED AND HATTED"

Many old Wiltshire cottages are made of porous chalk blocks and had to have "sarsen foundations, for the boots" and a "good hat" of thatch. Both served to keep out the damp and proved very effective.

THOMAS BOULTER

Thomas Boulter was one of the most notorious and best-loved of Wiltshire's highwaymen and his story has become legend.

He was the son of a Poulshot miller suspected of knavery, and, after being whipped in Devizes Market Place, was sentenced to death, later commuted to transportation. His mother, too, suffered whipping in Devizes, and it may be that this degredation nurtured a resentment in her son's mind and caused him to seek revenge and embark on a career of crime.

In 1775 Boulter set out, "armed with the artillery of a gentleman of the road," to rob. His first venture, on the road to Salisbury, was successful, and he was soon in possession of £40 and seven watches before returning to Poulshot.

He soon became known as the "Flying Highwayman of Wiltshire," but after a while became too conspicuous in the south and went to Ripon. There he was over-matched by a gentleman and his servant, tried at York Assizes and sentenced to death. This might well have been the end of his career had he not been offered a free pardon on the morning of execution if he joined His Majesty's army. He willingly agreed and for a few days he was seen "practising the goose step and submitting to the raps of the corporal's cane."

This became tedious and he deserted, and at Bristol formed an alliance with another rogue, James Caldwell, which eventually brought them side by side on the gallows.

Boulter "operated" all over the south of England, refreshing his horse with wine whenever he stopped for similar replenishment himself. A reckless man, he was always well dressed, and took care to be remembered by the waiters at inns where he was treated as a gentleman. On one of his robberies he was shot at close range and his left eye was permanently discoloured making him easily recognisable.

Boulter was arrested in Birmingham while attempting to sell some of his stolen goods and taken to Clerkenwell Prison in London. He escaped shortly afterwards leaving his irons suspended on a whitethorn bush!

It was due to the avarice of an innkeeper hoping to gain a large reward that Boulter was finally arrested and taken to Winchester gaol.

In August 1779, after a trial and confession, he was hanged at Winchester Castle with his friend Caldwell.

Although it is nearly two hundred years since his death, Boulter outlives all other Wiltshire highwaymen as the "unrivalled possessor of the combined qualifications which go to make up the accomplished freebooter who could rob at will yet shrank from the shedding of blood."

He steadfastly avoided murder and his memory is kept alive in his native Wiltshire, particularly in Poulshot where, maybe, his ghost rides still.

BOX

The shortest name place in the county and once called "the last place in Wiltshire on the way to Bath", there were once extensive stone quarries here. These were used for Isambard Brunel's great works on the old Great Western Railway.

The famous Box Tunnel, with its fine entrances, is considered one of the engineer's greatest designs. When it was first constructed, it was the longest railway tunnel in the world. It was very much distrusted by travellers, many of whom preferred to go "post" by horse along the road between Box and Corsham to avoid it!

THE BOY BISHOP

Long, long ago, St Nicholas' Day, the 6th December, was observed as a great festival in the Church, and Salisbury Cathedral was no exception.

Here, it was celebrated by a strange ceremony, that of choosing, from among the choristers, a "Boy Bishop." This mock Bishop, whose term of office lasted for three weeks, between St Nicholas' Day and the feast of the Holy Innocents on the 28th December, enacted a series of elaborate pageants and conducted all services.

If he died during this time, he was buried with the full honours of a bishop. Folk tradition claims that a miniature effigy of a bishop in the cathedral is that of a boy bishop who died in office, in spite of denials by historians.

BRADFORD OF THE SAXONS

Aptly named a melody of stone, Bradford on Avon stands on a steep hill with the River Avon flowing into the valley, and is one of the most delightful towns in the county, indeed, one of its proud inheritance.

There is so much to offer, and so much has been said and written about it, it is hard to particularise. Originally another of the weaving towns of Wiltshire, its Flemish weavers settled here in the reign of Edward III but the clothing industry has long disappeared, forced by the machine age to close the mills, though, to be fair, they continued until 1905 when rubber took the place of wool as the chief industry.

Obviously, the main attraction is the tiny church of St Lawrence, built one thousand years ago and the only complete Saxon Church in England. The church is believed to have been built by St Aldhelm and called "the purest Saxon Church in England," it stands, stark and bare, almost naked in its simplicity. It is as tall as it is long, and twice as high as it is wide. The chancel arch, the narrowest in England, is only three feet six inches, and the sculptured angels over the chancel arch are a very early example of church carving, said to be no later than the 10th century.

The "modern" church is Norman, and has a fifth century font. One of the first printed Bibles is preserved here.

In 1001, Bradford was given to the Abbey of Shaftesbury, and early in the 14th century a huge tithe barn was built. It is now one of the largest still existing in England and belongs to the nation. Fifty-five yards long, ten yards wide, it has fourteen great bays and four projecting gable porches. Its sturdy timbers bear up the span of the roof which extends to ten thousand square feet, and the barn is approached by a small bridge of the same age.

Bradford has an important Bridge over the Avon, originally a thirteenth century packhorse bridge which was enlarged in the fifteenth century. There are nine arches and a fourteenth century chapel which was later converted into a lockup with a domed roof and weather vane in the shape of a fish. A local saying describing occupants of the lockup was that they were "under the fish and above the water."

A harmony of old and new, Bradford has a rich inheritance with many houses of distinction. It is a place of underground streams and water perpetually tumbling from Ladywell, once the only source of water apart from the river. It has kept pace with modernity though, in no way, lost faith with its history.

BRADLEY OF THE MAIDENS

In the twelfth century, Manasser Biset, Steward to Henry II, founded a hospital here for "poor women lepers" thus giving this attractive village the name of Maiden Bradley. Later, a priory was founded which continued long after there was no need for the leprosy hospital, and, though long since crumbled into decay, remnants are there as a reminder at Priory Farm.

The pretty village is also the home of one of the County's ancient Ducal families — the Somersets, for it is the home of the Duke of Somerset, his family having lived here for generations.

A wayside fountain, dated 1891, presented by a Duke who provided the water, has the words:

Drink, travellers, drink of Bradley's purest rill
Which, strange to say, runs quite a mile up hill;
Then to your panting steeds let all attend,
An honest horse is surely man's best friend.

On an unhappier note, Maiden Bradley is the birthplace of Edmund Ludlow, the Parliamentarian General who was a member of the Court that tried and condemned Charles I. After the Restoration in 1660, he left the country, with other Regicides and died in exile in Switzerland.

THE REVEREND JOHN BRINSDEN

Sleeping peacefully in the churchyard of Winterbourne Monkton is the Reverend John Brinsden who was Vicar there when he died in 1719. He was buried at the east end of the churchyard with a sarsen stone from his own glebe placed over the grave.

In the spring, the numerous snowdrops to be seen there were originally planted by him in the form of letters of the alphabet, for the purpose, so he said of enlivening the dullness of the hornbook to the young children of his parish school.

THE BRUDERHOF

Ashton Keynes is the setting for a very unusual community in England. The Cotswold Bruderhof, of various nationalities, but mainly Germans driven from their own land, formed a community here — the first of its kind in England.

This Brotherhood of peaceful minded people — about two or three hundred in number — share a farm of three hundred acres. They live a self-contained life, receiving no wages and spending no money. They are self-sufficient, undertaking printing, book-binding and other work with their own small power station.

The community have over a hundred head of cattle, a hospital and whatever is necessary for the life of a small community.

It is interesting to reflect that, out of the whole of England, they chose to begin their new life in Wiltshire.

BURGLARS IN THE WILDERNESS

Long, long ago a gang of burglars at Marlborough College were terrorised into submission in the wilderness behind C House by a brave Watchman.

Tradition has it that these men were trying to steal a peacock when the Watchman hid behind a corner of C House, and, when the men were not looking, shouted "Boo" very loudly, upon which "they all fell down on their faces like gardeners in *Alice in Wonderland*". They were promptly marched off to prison and the peacocks strutted freely and happily on the green lawns.

CASTLE COMBE

This village, lying in a wooded ravine with a river running through it and grey limestone cottages to enhance the scene, was voted the "prettiest village in England" and is so well known that any description seems superfluous.

Throughout the centuries, it has kept its old world charm, and was once a weaving centre. The Weaver's House, where villagers took their cloth, after weaving it at home, still stands. The old cloth Market Cross is still the focal point of the village which has old inns and a 15th century church with a fine effigy of a knight in 13th century armour.

The river, Bybrook, is crossed by an ancient Pack Bridge, known in 1458 as the great "town bridge" and the village is rich in history with old houses in number. A wattle and daub gaol used at one time by the local constable, now has a new use — as a garden shed!

In the church, the priest's door is one of the smallest in England, measuring about five feet in height and two feet across!

CHEESE

The north of Wiltshire, especially the rich pasturelands in the Swindon area were particularly good for dairy farming, and, in the past, Wiltshire was known for its cheese-making.

Amesbury Abbey records in 1753 that Truckle Cheddar type cheeses were made in this area, about 9 lbs in weight. Traditionally, the cheeses ripened in lofts above the dairies of the farmhouses, so, when mature, the houses would be filled with the aroma of luscious food! Nowadays, some farms still make their own cheese, but, as a cheese producing area, Wiltshire no longer ranks with its neighbours.

CHEESECAKES

In reality a pastry, the Devizes Cheesecake is a delicacy peculiar to Wiltshire and to Devizes in particular.

Since the beginning of the 19th century, cheesecakes have been made by Strong's Restaurant from a very special recipe handed down from a Mrs Bowden and a Mrs Hook to the Strong family who continued to make them for two generations.

The cheesecake consists of a pastry, a curd base of junket, topped with fruit and spice and is delicious — unique to both town and county.

THE CHERHILL GANG

England in the eighteenth century was a lawless place, and Wiltshire was no exception.

The notorious Cherhill gang, a collection of footpads who terrorised travellers round the Calne area were much feared.

The Reverend Plenderleath, one time Vicar of Cherhill wrote of their activities at first hand.

"My own uncle, who was born in 1776, when he heard of my having accepted a living in Wiltshire, solemnly exhorted me never to think of driving across the downs without my servant and myself being provided with firearms.

"There was a band of footpads known as the "Cherhill Gang" who relieved many a traveller of the pence with which he intended to pay his scores owing at the Bell or Black Horse. Two old men who were said to have been members of this Society lived on into my period of residence, and anyone noticing their venerable white heads bowed over their prayer-books would have taken them for very Village Patriarchs thus ending their simple and blameless lives."

Tradition claims that one of the Gang is reported to have gone out on his marauding expedition in the summertime without a stitch of clothing! He said that not only did such an apparition frighten people on a dark night, but a naked man was less easily recognised than one who appeared in the ordinary clothes of the period.

CHRISTMAS PIE 1770

The following Wiltshire recipe for a Christmas pie in 1770 perhaps is indicative of the high standard of living of those days, or the keen air of the County gave everyone an appetite!

Ingredients:

2 Bushels of flour
20 pounds of butter
4 geese
2 turkeys
4 wild ducks
2 woodcocks
2 snipes
4 partridges
2 neats' tongues
2 curlews
7 blackbirds
6 pigeons

CHURCHES

For its size, Wiltshire is very well endowed with churches — over three hundred in all, many of them historical and with a claim to note.

In a county where religion has flourished for centuries, some saying pre-christianity had a hand in fashioning a sacred place at Stonehenge, there have been some remarkable churches, monasteries and religious orders over the centuries.

A very great many of the churches are old — there is the tiny Saxon church at Bradford-on-Avon, and countless churches with Norman features. The simplest church plan is to have a nave and chancel only, the word "nave" from the Latin, *navis* (ship) reminds one that the Church is a refuge on life's troubled waters.

The great Cathedral at Salisbury dominates the diocese, but there are churches with special associations or features which makes any selection impossible. The choice, therefore, must be personal and I have written of those churches that have attracted me. For this I make no apology, and it is a matter of regret that, in a book of this nature, it was not possible to include them all — for they would fill a book of their own. One that perhaps deserves a word for its originality is the church of Alderton which is said to be "imitation Norman and early English" and was built for a millionaire!

AN OLD CIDER PRESS

In a place so steeped in history as Avebury it is inevitable that there should be ghosts.

The Red Lion, the old coaching inn, standing near the circle, is said to be haunted. The story goes that, at midnight, the sound of a coach and horses can be clearly heard drawing up on the cobblestones outside the hotel. However, when the door is opened, nothing is there, and no one has ever reported actually seeing the coach.

Maybe one explanation is that the ghostly vehicle stops for refreshment. In the forecourt stands the remains of a very old cider press. The stone base shows the channels through which the juices ran during pressing, and the original wood and metal framework remain as a reminder of an old art.

COAT-OF-ARMS

The Wiltshire Coat-of-Arms was granted by the College of Arms to the County in 1937.

It consists of a Barry of eight argent and vert on a canton of the first a dragon rampant gules, and, for the crest, on a wreath of the colours, a bustard, wings elevated and addorsed proper.

The shield is simple in design, but neat, attractive and full of meaning. It embraces both geographical and natural history motifs. The green and white horizontal bands represent the many acres of fields and chalk downs. In the top left hand of the shield is a dragon which rears menancingly — an association with ancient Wessex. The bird which forms the crest is the mighty Great Bustard, a species extinct in this county about 1800, but, happily, now returned to their old haunts on Salisbury Plain.

THE COLUMN

In the heart of Savernake Forest, about a mile from "Tottenham House" (now Hawtreys School) stands a conspicuous monument known as "The Column". It was erected in 1781 by Thomas Brudenell-Bruce, first Earl of Ailesbury in "commemoration of the various benefits conferred upon him by his Uncle, Charles, Earl of Ailesbury and Elgin, and by his Sovereign, King George the Third."

All very commendable. But the story does not end there.

In 1788, King George the Third was seized with a violent malady and an inscription to this effect was added to the pedestal of the column. When the King's convalescence was announced in 1789, the loyal Marquis added yet another tablet to his column, reading:

"In commemoration of a signal instance of Heaven's Providence over these Kingdoms in the year 1789, *by restoring to perfect health, from a long and afflicting disorder, our excellent and beloved Sovereign, George the Third."*

A few months after his restoration to health, the King paid a visit to Savernake, accompanied by his Queen and three of the Royal Princesses. They had also visited Longleat, "whence they arrived at Savernake by way of Devizes and Marlborough on Wednesday, September 16th, 1789."

CORSHAM COURT

The Elizabethan Manor, home of the Methuen family, was much altered in the eighteenth century by Capability Brown who tried to create an Elizabethan mansion with Georgian features!

Corsham was a Royal Manor in Saxon times, coming into possession of the Methuen family in 1745.

Capability Brown designed the gardens with the customary lake and avenues and some fine trees were planted, and there is also the Bath house, designed for Dr Oliver, who, it was said, liked a cold plunge!

Two ice-houses, used for storing ice underground during the hot weather were made in the 1760s and are in existence today.

The house contains exceptional collections of pictures and furniture of the eighteenth century.

The Riding School, in the grounds, was used as a temporary church for the village when restorations to its own building were carried out from 1876 to 1878.

CRICKLADE FRUMENTY

Cricklade is an interesting place to the north of the county, with its church visible for miles across the landscape. The old part of the town is within a square enclosure, the boundaries of which follow the lines of ancient fortifications. Alfred is believed responsible for these, though Roman and Saxon sherds have been found among the footings.

Once described as the English "national food" frumenty is a very old dish traditionally served at certain times of year. Mothering Sunday was a particular occasion when it was made and Christmas another festive occasion when it graced the table.

Here is a recipe:
Barely cover half a pint of wheat with water and simmer until tender. This may take about twenty-four hours, or even longer. Pour on two pints of milk, add eight ounces of raisins with sugar and spice to taste. Bring to the boil and then simmer for an hour. Stir in two beaten eggs and serve hot.

CROFTON PUMPS

About three miles north-east of Burbage is the village of Crofton.

A pumping station there was built in 1800 to maintain the level of the water in the canal at its summit and two beam engines were installed in 1809 and 1812. The latter engine is now the oldest beam engine in the world which is still in working order.

THE DABCHICK

Long, long ago the villagers of Aldbourne were startled to see a strange bird in the middle of their pond.

None of them had ever seen such a bird before and they walked round and round staring at it.

In desperation, they sent for the oldest inhabitant, a man so old he had to be wheeled there in a barrow, and asked his advice. After he had been wheeled round three times, he said, "It's a dabchick."

Ever afterwards, the inhabitants of Aldbourne were known as dabchicks!

The association between the village and the bird is a long one, for some of the earliest bells cast at the foundry there bear the engraving of a small dabchick. These date from the reign of James I.

THE DEAD HORSE OF WOTTON RIVERS

In the long ago, all corn was carried by road which was a slow, laborious business. Sometimes, if the journey was a long one, the carter had to start in the middle of the night and travel through darkness.

On one such journey, a man left Manor Farm, Wootton Rivers, soon after midnight, to take a wagon of corn to Devizes. Three horses drew the load, and they had not gone very far when, just as they came to a bend in the road, the front horse dropped dead. The other two animals were besides themselves with fear. They stood trembling and nothing the carter could do would induce them to proceed on the journey. At last, he gave up and turned their heads towards their stable and they at once set off homewards at a brisk pace.

Next day, the body of the dead horse was examined but no one could discover the cause of death, the only clue being a piece of thick straw found on its back. The story goes that if the man had beaten the horse across this straw hard enough to draw blood, the spell would have been broken, for this straw was a witch who had taken that form. Maybe she was the witch who lived at Goblin's Hold, and whose face was seen at her window by many people long after she was said to be dead.

DEATH IN THE BRIDEWELL

The Old Bridewell, in the street of the same name in Devizes, has long been disused as a place of confinement, though the stout, studded oak door remains to this day.

An account of one occupant, published in 1788 is a melancholy one. "A prisoner named Thomas Platt, lately died in one of the solitary cells in the Bridewell, and the verdict of the Coroner's jury was — Died by hunger and cold."

After this sad occurrence, the allowance was augmented, but it was felt the place was unsuitable for a jail as it was much too small.

THE MANOR OF HUMPHREY DE BOHUN

The long, straggly village of Seend was once the manor of Humphrey de Bohun who fortified it in the fourteenth century, and it belonged to Lord Berners who was at the Field of the Cloth of Gold.

Henry VII encouraged some Flemish weavers to settle there, but they preferred the water of Trowbridge for their weaving and left. However, they stayed long enough to add a beautiful aisle to the church which stands on the brow of a hill, set in woodland and facing a picturesque valley.

In a moulding round the west window, John Stokys, a clothier, left his mark — a pair of shears — and he and his wife are commemorated in brass portraits on the wall.

HUBERT DE BURGH

In the twelfth century, Devizes was a turbulent place, much torn by strife and the struggles between rival claimants to the throne of England, one of whom, Matilda, is said to have escaped from Devizes Castle in a coffin disguised as a corpse!

Devizes became a royal castle, and, in the reign of Henry III, Hubert de Burgh, the great Justician, fell foul of the King's enemies and was incarcerated in Devizes castle in 1233.

A rumour reached de Burgh that his old adversary, the Bishop of Winchester, was plotting his death, so he took sanctuary in St John's church. To do so, he leapt from the castle wall, loaded with chains and fetters. Landing on some soft brambles and made his escape to the nearby church.

His enemies removed him by force from the church, though, it is said, he clung most desperately to the cross. The Bishop of Salisbury, on learning of this outrage, was furious and hastened to Devizes to secure de Burgh's release and return to sanctuary. The request was refused so his captors were excommunicated.

At last the other bishops took up the cause and de Burgh was returned to the church, though closely guarded. However, relief was at hand, for one Gilbert Bassett of Compton and a band of Lord Pembroke's men, routed the guards, freed de Burgh and took him to safety in Wales. Later, he regained his estates and died peacefully at Blackfriars.

REGINALD DE COBHAM

One of the followers of John Wycliffe to suffer in Wiltshire in 1413 was Reginald de Cobham, young lord of the manor of Langley Burrell.

The teachings of Wycliffe were held to be heretical and Reginald was condemned to die. He was taken to the top of Steinbrook Hill and slowly roasted to death.

Legend says that his naked ghost walks around the hill at midnight, when the moon is full, and, somewhat surprisingly, as he was burnt to death, is said to carry his head under his arm.

DEVIL'S DEN, FYFIELD

This ancient and curious dolmen, said to have been the inner chamber of a long disused barrow, was, in time past, covered with earth and ploughed into the surrounding fields. Only the stones remain, the uprights supporting the mushroom-like topping stone and for centuries they have defied wind and weather alike.

Tradition says that the devil appears occasionally, at midnight, with a team of white oxen and tries to pull it down. So far, he has not succeeded.

DEVIZES PIE

This traditional Wiltshire dish, once very popular, is now seldom seen and rarely served, even in large houses.

To make it, you would need :—

Sliced cold lamb
Slices of cold cooked calf's head
Calf's brains
Sliced tongue
Rashers of bacon

These meats were put into a piedish with some sliced, hard-boiled eggs, cayenne pepper, spice and salt, then covered with a stock that would set into a jelly. Lastly, the whole would be covered by pastry crust. Baked for about an hour, it was served cold — and delicious!

DEWPONDS

Living in a chalky environment, Wiltshiremen, had, long ago, to find a means of making artificial ponds for their stock.

The Smith family from Market Lavington were said to be the greatest of the Wiltshire dewpond makers, and made one of the last in 1938 for a chalk farmer on top of a high, bleak down.

The method of making these ponds was a jealously guarded secret, passed from family to family, but, first of all, there had to be a big hollow. This was packed with puddled clay, followed by a layer of lime, then straw, topped with stones and rubble. The whole was rammed down — hard!

Then, the first rainfall was awaited. This started the pond, and nightly dew kept it cool because of its construction.

The work of these skilled pond makers endures to this day and, often on the downs, a dewpond still provides sweet refreshment for the thirsty.

DOLE STONES

By no means uncommon in medieval times were doles paid either in bread or money. They often accompanied the Celebration in the Parish Church of an *obit* or yearly remembrance of some departed benefactor.

A massive erection, resembling a high tomb, sometimes found near the church porch is supposed to have been used for distributing these doles.

Examples are common in Wiltshire and are to be found in the churchyards of Potterne — near the south porch; Poulshot, near the south porch, Bradford on Avon and St Mary's, Devizes close to a south doorway in the chancel which is now blocked up.

This doorway is of fourteenth century origin and traditionally known as"The Founder's Tomb" but, on its removal some years ago, no traces of a burial were found. The same was also the case with the Potterne example.

A DOOM PAINTING

In a city dominated by its great Cathedral it is easy to overlook some of the other churches in Salisbury.

One of its three parish churches, St Thomas', stands in a churchyard surrounded by many gabled and tile-hung old houses. It was built in 1258 as a wooden chapel for the "benefit of the first inhabitants of New Sarum" and later built as a stone church.

The tower c. 1400 first stood detached from the church, but when the nave was rebuilt in the fifteenth century, it was joined to it, and its east face bears two quarter-jacks in armour dating from 1581.

However, the church's most famed possession is the Doom Painting over the chancel arch. Dating from 1400, the architectural background to the picture is remarkable. It was covered up at the time of the Reformation when Royal Arms, now over the south door, were placed over the chancel arch.

For centuries, the painting hung forgotten until, in the nineteenth century, it was uncovered and restored, and since that time has been a source of amazement to its beholders.

The painting of figures on either side of the chancel arch represent St Osmund on the south side and either St James of Compostella, or a pilgrim, who caused the painting to be placed there to commemorate his safe return from a pilgrimage.

The organ was presented to the Cathedral by George III but transferred to St Thomas' in 1877.

DOUBLE TRAGEDY AT FAIR

The church register for the tiny parish of Britford in the Avon valley records a double tragedy which took place in the year 1653.

Two women are buried in the churchyard because of an incident that took place at Salisbury Fair. The first woman died from a box on the ear — and the woman who struck the fatal blow was hanged.

THE DRUMMER BOY

The sad legend of the Drummer Boy (told in *Ingoldsby Legends*) originated in West Lavington where the boy's ghost is still said to appear.

In the 1770s, a drummer boy was murdered by a colour sergeant for his pay on Salisbury Plain, where the Lavington road joins the main Devizes road.

Some years later the sergeant was walking at the scene of the murder when he thought he heard the sound of drumming and imagined he saw the drummer boy he had so callously murdered. He was so frightened that he confessed his crime and was later hanged.

Though the sergeant paid for his crime, it is said the sound of drumming can still be heard on that lonely road to Salisbury.

STEPHEN DUCK

Charlton is a small village which came under Royal notice through a man called Stephen Duck who was born there in 1705.

As a young man he became a thresher, a mower and a reaper and then a poet. His work so interested Queen Caroline she became his patron.

The Queen so liked his poems she listened to them in her drawing room at Windsor, gave him an annuity, and other honours before having him educated for the Church. In 1752 she gave him the rectory of Byfleet.

Unfortunately, he drowned himself in the River Kennet at Reading in 1756, but is still remembered in his native village.

The Charlton Duck Supper which is an unique village festival is held annually on June 1st. This is attended by twelve men, one of whom is the Chief Duck and wears a ceremonial cap, and a toast is drunk in memory of Stephen Duck and Lord Palmerston. The funds for the feast were provided from the rent of a field donated by Lord Palmerston.

So the thresher who became a poet is not forgotten.

A DUMBLEDORE

Wiltshire folk often like to give nicknames to animals and insects and, to them, a bumblebee is known as a dumbledore.

However, superstition regarding bees is still strong in the county, and many still believe that a beekeeper should "tell the bees" of any family event, particularly favoured is the custom of telling them of the death of the owner of the colony. If the bees were not told, it was believed all the bees in the hive would also die. It was also usual (and patriotic!) to tell the bees when the Sovereign died. Some said when this happened, they would fly all over the countryside, telling the birds and flowers as if to make all Nature acquainted with the tidings.

Another "bee" sign was that, if a swarm settled on dry wood, it was a certain sign of death in the owner's family. Long ago, at Basset Down, a labourer's daughter was lying ill and a swarm of bees alighted on some dry wood. Nothing could reassure the girl's mother who was sure it was a sign of death. Next day, her daughter died.

AN EARLY BISHOPRIC

The village of Ramsbury or "Raven's fortified place" as its name implies, was once a place of considerable historical interest for it was one of the seats of the Wiltshire Bishopric in the tenth century. The See was transferred to Old Sarum in 1075, but, happily, in 1974, the Bishopric was revived, and there is, once more, a Bishop of Ramsbury.

The very impressive church, partly built on Saxon foundations, with shafts of crosses and grave covers dating the 9th century, dominates the village. One ninth century cross shaft depicts a serpent biting its tail and is executed in Viking style. Along his back is a double line of chevron designs.

A huge elm, centuries old and now completely hollow is some twenty-one feet in circumference and forms a focal point. It is believed that, once, it formed part of Savernake Forest.

On a "modern" note, an old coaching inn bears the curious name of the Bleeding Horse, said to derive from the days when travelling vets lodged there.

Oliver Cromwell held one of his Councils there in the Civil War, though, luckily, his army did not destroy the church.

EARLY PROMISE, DEPRIVED OF FULFILMENT

The headstone, dated 1844, to a seven year old child who died at Donhead St Mary reads:

Gifts of grace and love of learning
Early in this youth combined
Blest with intellects discerning,
Open heart, and virtuous mind;
Hence his tender parents grieving,
Leave this tribute on his stone
Humbly hoping and believing
God in Christ accepts their son.

FAIR NELL

Place Farm at Tisbury was once owned by the Abbess of Shaftesbury. Among the nuns here, was Fair Nell, a very beautiful woman who committed the terrible sin of looking upon a man.

As a punishment, she was condemned to walk for ever in a tunnel that (supposedly) connected Place Farm with the top of the Ridge. Today there is a copse known as Farnell's Cope (Fair Nell's Copse). She is still walking.

Moonrakers have ever been inventive, and learnt to come to terms with their land and conditions, so it is not surprising that among its people are numbered two eminent farming pioneers.

One of them, John Fowler, was born in Melksham in 1826. His family were Quakers and his father was an Elder of the Society of Friends. At the age of seventeen, John worked in a flour milling business where he developed his love of mechanical pursuits.

The first steam plough he invented was "put to work on April 10th, 1856 on a farm at Nacton, the property of Sir George Brook."

Following the great success of this achievement, Fowler improved the steering of the implement and established a Steam Plough works at Leeds, where he died, in 1860, having made a substantial contribution to the success of farming in England.

One of his Ploughs was exhibited at the great Paris Exhibition, and, in 1868, ten thousand French farmers assembled to watch a demonstration. At the grand banquet which followed it was announced that Emporer Louis Napoleon had awarded a gold medal to the French firm who had brought the plough from England, and toasts were drunk to the memory of the Wiltshire inventor, John Fowler.

A more recent pioneer was the Wiltshire farmer, A. J. Hosier, who devised a portable milk bail. Under his, then, revolutionary, system, the milking machine and shed, complete with cake feeders and dairy, were taken to the cows in the fields instead of bringing the cows in for milking in the time-honoured fashion in the farmyard. The cows "lived out" as it were, became healthier, and also fertilised the soil.

FIELD FLEA-WORT

The small, uncommon, bright yellow wildflower — the Field Flea-Wort grows in profusion on the green, unfrequented Iron Age hillfort known as Liddington Castle near Swindon. Set in the Vale of the White Horse, above Swindon, the place was much frequented by the great naturalist, Richard Jefferies, and it is said, by some, the small flower grows there in his memory.

THE FINGER STOCKS

The seventeenth century was the time of many strange and cruel punishments, some often used in large houses for the correction of unruly servants.

These finger pillories or finger stocks as they are called usually consisted of two pieces of oak, the bottom and fired piece normally three feet long, the width of the whole being about four and a half inches. When closed it was five inches deep, and the left hand supported by a leg the same width as the top. The upper and lower pieces are joined by a hinge and in the lower and fixed horizontal part are a number of holes, varying in size, some being sufficiently large as to admit the finger as far as the second joint. When the fingers were imprisoned, the whole would be fastened shut and the hand could not be withdrawn until the pillory was opened. If an offender were held long in this position, it must have been extremely painful.

Littlecote House possesses one of the pillories said to have been used by Judge Popham to confine prisoners in the dock, though it may also have been used for unruly servants.

THE FIRST HOUSE OF CORRECTION

Wiltshire's first House of Correction was established at Devizes by 1579 and in 1606 was called "The Bridewell".

Over the years, this place deteriorated, and, in 1810, an imposing new prison was built on the Bath Road, using convict labour! It was completed in 1816 and of polygonal shape with the Governor's house occupying the centre.

This house overlooked all the yards and the building was very secure, with eleven wards and eleven yards, ten for men and one for women. The total number of cells was two hundred and ten, and were some ten feet high, seven feet wide and just over eight feet long.

An ingenious "anti-escape" plan was to place loose blocks on the nineteen foot high outer wall, so that these would be dislodged if any attempted freedom and raise the alarm.

A treadmill, for hard labour, was introduced in 1815 for grinding the corn used to make bread in the prison bakery. Prisoners dreaded the treadmill, for the hours were long and hard — 9½ in the summer and never less than 6 the rest of the year.

Over twenty thousand people witnessed the first public hanging of John Goodman and Edward Amor in 1824 on a gallows outside the prison gates. The last execution within the gates, was in 1903.

It was no longer used for convicted prisoners after 1911, it became a military detention barracks in 1914, but the military gave up possession in 1920.

No trace of this grim place now remains, and modern houses cover the area where so many suffered.

FIVE ALLS INNS

These are known in England, and Wiltshire is no exception, one being at Chippenham and another one at Marlborough. Of course the Five "Alls" are —

The King — I rule all
The priest — I pray for all
The lawyer — I plead for all
The soldier — I fight for all
The last — John Bull — I pays for all.

FLINT - KNAPPING

The Wiltshire craft of making flints for guns and tinder-boxes flourished in this county in the nineteenth century, due, probably to the ready availability of the materials.

The vast store of Neolithic barrows and tombs with their countless flint axe-heads were a treasure trove.

"Flint Jack" as he was called, was said to have been a "great rogue" but, maybe, he was just a good businessman who seized an opportunity when it was presented to him. He made many "Neolithic" flints himself and was a well known character.

FLYING SCHOOL

The silence of the turf of the plains made the area round Larkhill an ideal bird sanctuary — until the coming of the army! For years, the only sound that disturbed the tranquillity was the cry of the lapwing, or the sweet song of the skylark which gave the place its name. Happily, in spite of the intrusion of man, his guns and vehicles, the sound of the brave little birds can still be heard on a clear day.

Larkhill is remembered for another reason. In 1912 it was one of the pioneer flying centres, for, in 1909, the Bristol Tramway and Carriage Company had entered the, then infant, aircraft industry. It set up a flying school at Larkhill, and it was here that the "Boxkite," the first plane by the company's own designer, first took the air in 1910. Sixteen were soon built and used in the flying school.

In May 1912 an experimental tractor plane was abandoned after it overturned and ran into a crowd of spectators, but Larkhill airfield played its part in the development of Bristol planes, among them, the famous Scout.

The pioneer flying school closed in September 1914.

FOVANT

With a small river running by the village street, Fovant is in the south of the county with downs rising above it.

It was on these downs during the first World War that some Australian soldiers, to relieve their boredom while training, decided to cut something different into the chalk. No white horses for them — instead they laboriously carved out reminders of their homeland and a map of Australia, a kangaroo and a rising sun appeared on the chalkland. Later, Regimental badges were to be seen. Every summer an annual service is held here.

A GHOSTLY INTERVENTION

Early seventeenth century Wiltshire was the scene of a very strange happening. The story is that, Sir Walter Long, Member of Parliament, of Draycot Cerne, was persuaded by his second wife to hire a lawyer and change his Will to prevent his son, John, the rightful heir from inheriting the property.

Legend says that each time the lawyer's hand began to write the fateful clause, a lady's hand appeared between the candle and the parchment on which he was writing. The lawyer, taking this to be a Divine warning, refused to complete the deed, and another was called in. The hand was believed to be that of Sir Walter's first wife, protecting the interests of her son:

The sequel was that a compromise was reached — Sir Walter retaining the Draycot property, and his son taking another at Wraxall, thus dividing the estate. The ghostly hand has not been seen again.

THE ONLY GIANT IN ENGLAND

Salisbury Plain is at the heart of the earliest known civilisation in England, so it is natural that ancient customs and beliefs have been handed down to succeeding generations, many from pre-Christian beliefs.

One of the most striking of physical survivals of custom and legend is the Giant in Salisbury Museum. The only Giant now left in the whole of this country, he stands, some twelve feet high, with dark complexion, bushy black hair and whiskers and huge, staring eyes.

His robes are large enough to hide his bearer when

he moves in procession through the Salisbury streets, beside him his Hob-nob, or hobby horse, and his sword, lantern and staff.

In medieval times, the Giant was known as St Christopher, possibly because the Saint was known to have been a giant, and, as the patron saint of travellers, many believed that if they looked on his image, they would travel safely.

Salisbury Giant belongs to a pre-Christian time linked with the Midsummer Festival, and, in the Middle Ages was appropriated by the Tailors' Guild whose patronal festival was on June 24th.

The Giant's real age is uncertain, but there is evidence that he was in the procession led by the Mayor and Corporation to meet Henry VII and his Queen in 1496, and he was old at that time.

During the Commonwealth, when all merriment was frowned upon, the Giant and Hob-nob remained in obscurity to re-appear at the restoration of King Charles II with much rejoicings.

Now the Giant and Hob-nob are really old and frail and appear only at coronations, waiting meanwhile, in honourable retirement.

GILBERTINE CONVENT

Twelfth century Marlborough was the seat of a Gilbertine House. This order of nuns, was founded by Gilbert of Sempringtom in 1148, and was the only order of English origin that did not spread outside the country. In Marlborough, the house flourished in 1190 and was probably the eleventh or twelfth of this particular order to be formed in England. The buildings have long since vanished, though there is a house still known as The Priory.

GLORY BE TO GOD

The little village of Wootton Rivers bridges the Kennet and Avon Canal east of Pewsey and is a pleasant enough place, possessing a strange and unusual clock.

The fourteenth century church of St Andrew was restored in the 1860s but, until the coronation of King George V, lacked a clock. To commemorate this national event, the village wanted to add a clock to their church, but the idea was abandoned because of the cost.

Then, a local craftsman, Jack Spratt, came forward with a novel idea. He said he would make the clock himself! He asked for a few hundred weights of metal, any old scraps of iron, steel, lead or brass and the villagers rallied round, presenting him with old bicycles, bedsteads and the like. The pile grew and soon there were enough old prams, pipes, cutters and reaping machines to make the clock.

At first, it was thought the wheel and pinions would come from a London firm but the castings were eventually made by a Pewsey factory using wooden patterns, making the clock truly a Wiltshire effort.

In place of figures, Jack Spratt spelt out the words GLORY BE TO GOD, and the hands, which are exposed, are ingeniously protected from the weather.

Jack Spratt's memorial — a labour of love so freely given — is a source of wonder to visitors and residents alike.

A WILTSHIRE GLOSSARY

Wiltshire, as other counties, has some words that are their own invention and known only to true Moonrakers. Here is a sample:

AGG — to irritate
BLACK - BOB — a cockroach
BLADES — the shafts of a wagon
BORSY — coarse
CAG - MAG —inferior meat
CHARM — hounds in full cry
COME OF — get the better of
DRATTLE — much talk
FALLING — a downfall of snow (only used for snow)
GARLEY - GUT — gluttonous person
GLUTCHER — the throat
HUD — the skin of a gooseberry, shell of a pea or bean
JIFFLE — confusion
LOPPETTY — weak, out of sorts
LUCE — lukewarm
MISTPOND — a dewpond
MUGGLE — live in haphazard way
PIG MEAT — never pork, unless animal killed as "little porker"
QUILL A PERSON — to humour them
SKIMMER CAKE — made of scraps of dough
TEG - MAN — a shepherd

THE GODOLPHIN SCHOOL

Founded in 1726, the Godolphin School at Salisbury is one of the oldest girls' schools in England, and the City is justly proud of its presence on Milford Hill. The girls, distinctive with their straw boaters and scarlet hatbands, are as much a feature of the City scene today as in their early days.

Elizabeth Godolphin, its founder, was the wife of Charles Godolphin, her cousin, and the daughter of Francis Godolphin of Coulston, and a member of the distinguished family which rendered much service to England over the centuries.

Charles Godolphin was brother to the Lord High Treasurer of Great Britain, and he and his wife are commemorated on a tablet in the cloisters of Westminster Abbey. In her Will, Elizabeth decreed that a school be founded for "educating eight young orphan gentlewomen" and from this nucleus, a great school began.

As time passed, the school grew and prospered with many famous women listed in the annals of its Old Girls. Today, there are over three hundred pupils, some boarders and others, day girls or "Sarums" as they were nicknamed.

The year 1926 was the Bicentenary and much celebrated. Westminster Abbey was the focal point with a special Service of Thanksgiving in the cloisters near the memorial tablet to Elizabeth Godolphin on the 24th June 1926. A bunch of red and white peonies (the school colours) was placed at the foot of the tablet.

In the presence of a huge gathering, "the School marched in, in orderly ranks, holding their heads high," with Miss Ash, the Head Mistress, followed by her staff. The Head Girl, Betty Luckham, held the wreath and another girl carried the Godolphin banner with the Godolphin arms. The processions of Old Girls and past members of the staff and the presence of some distinguished visitors, completed the assembly. Then, the Deans of Salisbury and Westminster entered and the simple, but impressive, service began.

The hymns included one of thanksgiving, "Now thank we all our God," prayers of gratitude and endeavour, the stirring call to "Fight the good Fight," and a blessing.

In the Abbey at Evensong that night, the girls attended the service, when special prayers were said for the School, the ceremonies ended with the hymn, "For all the Saints,"

Perhaps some of those who took part thought of Elizabeth Godolphin and thanked her for her forethought and generosity in providing this rather special place of learning.

As an old girl, I look back on my days there with mixed feelings. I will always remember my Confirmation in the great Cathedral, and the feeling of hope it gave me. I believe my time at the School gave me a sense of values and a standard of living to which I will always strive.

THE GOOD OLD DAYS

Extract from a Wiltshire Housekeeping Account of 1778.

	£	s	d
Butter, 6 lbs.		4	0
Two couples of fowls		2	6
Two turkeys		10	0
3 hams	1	13	0
Two pigs (probably suckling pigs)		7	6
Salmon, 7 lbs.		7	0
1 gallon currants		1	0
1 quarter of lamb		2	4
9 lbs. veal		2	8
15 lbs cheese		5	7
20 lbs. honey		12	3

GREAT BUSTARDS

In bygone years, Salisbury Plain was famous for its Great Bustards. These magnificent birds, like great turkeys and weighing up to thirty pounds, once roamed freely on the wide, open spaces of Wiltshire.

Like autumn flocks, they traversed the green swirl of the Plain, and from a distance, they resembled flocks of sheep, or as some said, fallow deer. They were not easy to kill, for their wings were strong and they were wary, cunning birds. Ploughing and enclosure finally drove them from Wiltshire and by 1800 they were uncommon.

For over 140 years, they have been extinct in Britain, but ornithologists were delighted when, a couple of years ago, they re-established themselves at Porton Down. Some thirteen birds appeared and it is hoped these numbers will increase and once again the Great Bustard will be a common sight on the Plain.

THE GREAT CATHEDRAL

For a county so richly endowed with fine churches, it might be excused if the Cathedral were in the same mould as so many up and down England.

Wiltshire is different! Salisbury Cathedral is one of the most impressive and magnificent in England. Set in a perfect setting of lush green lawns and sheltering houses contained in a tranquil Close. Wisely, the tombstones were removed years ago, leaving the approach plain and perfect from any angle.

The foundations were laid in 1220 and it was consecrated in 1258 in the presence of Henry III. One of the finest examples of its period, its magnificent spire rises to a height of four hundred and four feet, and was of course, immortalised by the Constable painting.

One of the few in England in the shape of a double Cross with the arms of the transept branching off on either side, it stands impressive in its grey magnificence.

In 1327 Edward III gave permission for stone from Old Sarum Cathedral to be used for the erection of a wall surrounding the Close, and the wall and gates still stand sentinel today.

The interior is another store-house of English treasure, perhaps one of the most interesting being the ancient clock mechanism, dating from 1386, the oldest piece of machinery still at work in Britain, maybe even in the whole world.

The monuments include the tomb of William Longespee who witnessed the sealing of the Magna Carta, and there is an original copy brought from Runnymede in June 1215 by the Earl of Salisbury who gave it to the Cathedral for safekeeping.

Long years ago, the shrine of St Osmund was the scene of pilgrimage when many came to be cured of their ills. The Audley Chantry, a tiny chapel at the east end, was said to have been used as a blacksmith's shop by Cromwell's Roundheads during the Civil War, but mercifully, they did not sack the building.

Brave and magnificent, Salisbury Cathedral has been a centre of Christian worship for centuries, and few could fail to be moved by its splendour and meaning. To attend a Service is an occasion to be remembered, when faith is renewed against a background in which the very stones seem to offer encouragement and endurance.

GREAT CHALFIELD

A delightful group of buildings standing reflected in the calm water of a moat is an accurate description of Great Chalfield. The village stands in lush, green fields watered by a stream, and it resembles a picture of country life in England when the church, manor and farm were the centre of each community.

Described as a "fine example of a medieval domestic house" the Manor has a forecourt approached by a great archway, and strong oak doors in parts of the house which, together with its moat, give to the house an air of fortification.

It was built in 1480, during the Wars of the Roses by Thomas Tropenell whose benefaction also included the lovely church and his arms are displayed on the roof and on the screen.

GREAT PORCH HOUSE

This fifteenth century, half-timbered house in an uneasy setting of a busy street in Devizes, is believed to have belonged to St John's Hospitallers.

With sturdy oak beams, oak door and carved faces protruding from the timbers, it is an unique example of medieval architecture as it contains two addiitional wings at the rear.

GREY WETHERS

Near Fyfield on the Marlborough Downs is a strange cluster of sarsen stones. From a distance, they resemble sheep because of the density and greyness of their appearance.

They are geological formations peculiar to this part of Wiltshire, really being the remains of a sort of sandstone deposited on the chalk long, long, long, ago when it was the bed of the sea at the beginning of time.

GROVELEY, GROVELEY

Few places in the country celebrate Oak Apple Day, May 29th, with more fervour than the inhabitants of Great Wishford.

This old custom, commemorating the ancient rights of the villagers to cut wood in Groveley Wood according to medieval manorial right, has links with pre-Christian tree worship.

In 1603, the villagers were granted the right to gather wood from Groveley wood for all time, and they ensure this privilege by their special celebrations.

The festivities begin by a vast gathering in the centre of the village. Everyone goes to the wood, accompanied by a band of musicians playing mouth organs, tin whistles, even saucepans! They return to the village, each carrying a branch, then process through the streets with a banner proclaiming, "Groveley, Groveley and all Groveley, Unity is Strength".

Dressed in old fashioned country style, a party go to Salisbury Cathedral where they dance on the green before the procession marches to the High Altar. There, the Rector of Wishford reads out the relevant part of the 1605 Charter setting out the villagers' rights to collect wood, the Chairman of the Oak Apple Club raises his white wand and everyone shouts, "Groveley, Groveley and all Groveley!"

Then, back to the villlage where the rest of the day is spent in celebrating with maypole dancing, music and singing.

QUEEN GUINEVERE

When the death of the lovely Queen Guinevere took place at Amesbury Abbey, there followed what must have been one of the most beautiful and tragic funeral processions in history. For two nights and the best part of two days, Sir Lancelot and his seven companions went on foot for the long, forty miles from "Almesbury (Amesbury) unto Glastonbury" escorting the bier upon which lay, her face uncovered, the body of Queen Guinevere.

Malory recounts that an hundred torches were ever burning about the corpse of the queen, and "ever Sir Lancelot with his seven fellows went back about the horse bier, singing and reading many an holy orison, and placed frankincense upon the corpse."

Who knows — if strength and poignancy of feeling are a cause of haunting one might still meet those figures on the long, long road of sorrow. But it is said the beautiful vision has been seen but once — on the first, tragic journey.

GULLIVER — THE SMUGGLER

In eighteenth century Wiltshire, there lived a man called Gulliver and this one was not renowned for his travels!

He was a Wiltshireman who organised a clever network of smuggling ranging over several counties. By about 1758, there were so many people involved that it made the work of the Excisemen almost impossible.

Gulliver settled at Thorney Down about ten years later and from there the smugglers' route led to Poole and back to Salisbury, via Handley. Ten years later, he moved again, to Kinson, to further his activities and Thorney Down was a rendezvous.

In middle-age, he retired to Lyme Regis and was said to have married a banker's daughter and lived in great comfort at Wimborne.

A HAWTHORN SUPERSTITION

Much used in cures, the hawthorn was considered to be the special tree of the witch. It had many uses in days gone by — its distilled water, made from the flowers, was thought to draw thorns and skin blisters. The creamy, white blossoms in Maytime, and the autumn red fruit — called haws — make an excellent wine, or were good — in tea — for heart conditions and dropsy. Some found an infusion of flowers good for sore throats.

Wiltshire folk feel it is unlucky to bring mayblossom into a house as it is said to mean a death, so it is rarely used in decoration, only medicinally. Possibly this stemmed from the time of the ancient Druids as legend recalls that a young maiden and young man were chosen as a perfect pair. For a year they were treated as a King and Queen, then ceremoniously put to death. The doomed couple were crowned with mayblossom.

MAUD HEATH'S GIFT

It is more than five hundred years since a market woman living near Chippenham grew tired of the difficulties of journeying to the weekly market and, using her life savings, directed that a causeway be built.

This causeway, about four and a half miles in length, stretches from the top of Wick Hill in Bremhill Parish to Chippenham, passing through Tytherton, Kellaways and Langley Burrell on the way.

Maud Heath was that market woman who walked every week from her home at Bremhill to Chippenham market selling eggs and poultry. At the bottom of the hill she had to struggle through one of the worst stretches of road in the county, mostly marsh and mud. She often fell and lost her eggs to say nothing of soiling her clothes. Being a resolute person, she decided that no one else should suffer as she had done, and, though it was the year 1474, she ordered that this causeway be made — a high, stone walk along which people have walked dry shod ever since.

The Causeway runs parallel with the lane, to the left for some 200 yards. The path is carried over a series of some 70 arches, each with a span of 7 feet and constructed of brick and stonework in-filled with flint. The grading was skilful so that the rise from the level of the lane at each end to the highest point — 6 feet in all, in the middle of the bridge, is hardly perceptible.

To make sure the causeway never fell into disrepair, she left a considerable sum of money to her trustees for its maintenance, and so it remains to this day, a fine memorial to a woman's determination.

The Deed of Gift by which Maud Heath gave land to Trustees is dated the 12th June 1474, and the income from the bequest has been used to make and maintain the causeway from Wick Hill to Chippenham. This original deed, still in the possession of the trustees, was found among some papers by the Rector of Delamere in 1871.

Medieval England, the England of Maud Heath, was a hard-working land in which the peasants toiled from dawn to dusk for little reward and the roads were non existent. They had to walk everywhere for there was no transport for the poor, and for recreation they relied on Miracle Plays, with the church as the focal point of life in the village. Fairs were often held in the churchyards, and the walls of the church decorated with pictures from the Bible to illustrate to the illiterate congregation the meaning of the words.

The original causeway was made of cobblestones, but later, limestone brash placed on edge was used to make a path which was most useful when the river was in flood.

Commemorative stones have been erected at intervals at the side of the causeway, the first of these being the statue on the top of Wick Hill where there is a fine view of the whole valley. Maud Heath, with her basket at her side, sits and looks for miles. The inscription reads:

Those who didst pause on their ariel height
Where Maud Heath's Pathway winds in shade or light
Christian wayfarer in a world of strife
Be still and ponder on the Path of Life,

On the opposite side of the road is a stone bearing the following:

From this Wick Hill begins the praise
Of Maud Heath's gift to these highways.

The causeway ends at Chippenham with a plate affixed to a stone on the opposite side of the Langley Road from St Paul's entrance. It is inscribed:

Hither extendeth Maud Heath's gift
From where I stand is Chippenham's Clift.
Erected 1698, *but given* 1474.

One may ask — how much did all this cost? The inscription on the pillar at Kellaways states that Maud Heath left "eight pounds a year" — not a large sum by today's standards, but in 1474, it indicated considerable wealth. There is some disagreement as to whether she was a widow or a spinster, some saying she was the widow of John Heath and possessed considerable wealth, but the version of the troubled market woman trudging along a muddy path to sell eggs, and so enraged by the soakings she endured, resolved to do something about it — and did! is perhaps the most appealing. One can the more easily picture her stumbling along, her clothes bespattered by mud, her feet in rough clogs, slipping and slithering until, unable to keep her balance, she fell, surrounded by a clutter of broken eggs and hens' feathers. Then, one day, she had had enough!

Her five hundredth anniversary was duly celebrated and, for another five hundred years, people will have cause to remember Maud Heath.

THOMAS HELLIKER

During the industrial strife in the nineteenth century, the town of Trowbridge, with its cloth mills was no exception, and when one manufacturer tried to instal machines in his factory workmen came to smash them.

Among them was a young cloth finisher, Thomas Helliker, who was only nineteen years of age. Information was given that he was the ringleader of the trouble and he was arrested and tried at Salisbury, where, though he protested his innocence, he refused to name his accomplices. He was adjudged guilty and hanged on his nineteenth birthday.

The clothworkers of Wiltshire were much impressed by the bravery and loyalty of their young colleague, and considered him a martyr to their cause. He is buried in Trowbridge churchyard and his tomb bears the following inscription, lovingly subscribed by his friends:

> *Sacred to the memory of Thomas Helliker, the thread of whose life was cut in the bloom of youth. He exchanged mortality for immortality, March* 22, 1803, *in the* 19*th year of his age.*
>
> *The fatal catastrophe which led to this unfortunate event is too awful to describe, suffice to say that he met death with greatest fortitude and resignation of mind. Considering his youth he may be said to have but few equals. He died a true penitent, being very anxious in his last moments that others might take a timely warning and avoid evil company.*
>
> *This tomb was erected at his earnest request by the clothmaking factories of the counties of Wilts and Somerset, as a token of their love and veneration for his memory.*

HERALDRY

There is much heraldry to be found in the cathedrals, churches and ancestral homes of this country, and Wiltshire is no exception. It is to be found on tombs and monuments of all periods, in stained-glass windows and carved carefully in stone and wood on walls, roofs, screens and stalls — even on fonts — while shields of a religious nature may be seen on altar hangings and other sanctuary furnishings.

Many churches dating from the fifteenth century have effigies of men in armour and Wiltshire possesses one of the most splendid of these. At Lydiard Tregoze church stands a life-size figure of a Cavalier in gilded armour, topped by a marble canopy. It is in memory of Edward St John killed in the Civil War, fighting for the King at Newbury.

Of the three hundred churches in the county, many date from Norman times and have their heritage of heraldic monuments and brasses. To list them all would be tedious — and there are special books to guide one through particular churches — so this book refers to some known to me.

Bromham Church is rich in heraldry and brasses, and its Chantry Chapel displays the arms of Roche, St Armand, Ashton, Braybrooke, Delamere and Anstie.

As might be expected, Lacock has a fine collection with over thirty coats of arms displayed dating from Norman times.

Bishops Cannings, Steeple Ashton (with its palimpsest brass), Broad Hinton, Aldbourne, Great Bedwyn, Corsham and so the list grows. Suffice it to say that Wiltshire does not lag behind other counties in its heraldic inheritance.

THE HIGHWAYMAN'S GRAVE

Half a mile or so west of Beckhampton is the site of what is known locally as the "Highwayman's Grave."

It is said he was trying to hold up the London to Bath stagecoach and was shot dead by the guard. He was buried face down, with his head to the west.

Gypsies believed he was a "traveller" not a highwayman at all, and for many, many years placed flowers on his grave.

HIGHWORTH

This old town is set high in the hills of north Wiltshire, and from the top of one of them you can see for three counties.

The fifteenth century church was fortified and held for the King in the Civil War, but was stormed by Fairfax, the dead soldiers being buried in a field nearby. The tower bears the marks of the battle, and by the west door there are three headless angels — possibly victims of the same war.

Many generations of the Warneford family are commemorated in the memorials, among them Lieutenant R. A. J. Warneford V.C. who shot down the first Zeppelin to be destroyed in flight in the first World War.

HORSEMAN'S GRAVE

Set high on the hills behind the village of Ogbourne St Andrew is a cross marking the resting place of Patrick Francis Hartigan who was buried here in 1921. It is known locally as the Horseman's Grave, and the verse on the pedestal reveals why:

Beneath the clean and spacious sky
Here let the sleeping horseman lie,
Nor from his darlings sunder;
And as the thoroughbreds flash by
This dust may quicken suddenly
To hear the gallops thunder.

HENRY HUNT

Born at Widdington Farm, Upavon, in 1773, this remarkable man was one of the most active and popular characters in England. Following the family tradition of farming, he was successful at Enford, regularly journeying to Devizes Market, where in 1795, he married Miss Halcombe of the Bear Inn there.

In 1801, he was very prosperous, his property, live and dead stock being valued at £20,000, and as proof of his patriotism, he voluntarily tendered the whole of this property to the Government in case of invasion. He also agreed that he, together with three servants and his valuable horses, should "make the first charge upon the enemy".

Due to a misunderstanding, he received a letter from Lord Bruce, saying his services in the Marlborough troop of yeomanry cavalry would no longer be required and requesting him to return his sword and pistols. Furious, Henry Hunt answered in person, demanding satisfaction! For this offence he was fined £1,000 and sentenced to six weeks' imprisonment. This set him on the political road and he unsuccessfully contested Bristol and Somerset.

Soon he became known as "Orator Hunt" and was chief speaker at an assembly of some 80,000 people near Manchester when the "Peterloo massacre" was perpetrated in 1819.

At length, he entered Parliament as Member of Parliament for Preston in 1830, and died at the age of 62 in 1835.

Henry Hunt was a remarkable man being "tall, muscular with a healthful complexion — a manly deportment, half yeoman and half sportsman."

When living on his farm he generally drove to Devizes market in a four-in-hand, and was so strong that he was able to do a day's work with any labourer in the county. Readiness rather than strength was the characteristic of his understanding, and many of what were considered his extreme views have since been embodied in legislation.

EDWARD HYDE, EARL OF CLARENDON

One of England's famous statesmen was born at Dinton House in February 1608, and, though he intended studying for the Church, circumstances led to his reading law. Entering the Middle Temple, he studied under Sir Nicholas Hyde, his uncle, and was a brilliant scholar. As a young man, he formed lasting friendships with some of the eminent men of the time and avoided those not renowned for talent and virtue.

In 1640 he became Member of Parliament for Wootton Bassett, and while loyal to the King, gained the confidence of the Commons.

During the Civil War, he joined the King's party and was nominated Chancellor of the Exchequer and a member of the Privy Council, being knighted for his services. After the battle of Naseby, he accompanied Prince Charles to Jersey, where he remained for two years writing his great work *The History of the Great Rebellion.*

At the Restoration of King Charles II, he returned to England as Lord Chancellor and was made a peer, taking the title of Earl of Clarendon. He was regarded as the King's first and most confidential minister.

His enemies plotted against him and an impeachment for high treason was commenced against him, but he fled to France where he died in 1674. He was eventually buried in Westminster Abbey.

RICHARD JEFFERIES

A true lover of the English countryside, Richard Jefferies, who was born in 1848, was the son of a Wiltshire farmer. He spent much of his youth wandering the beautiful Marlborough Downs and his descriptions of the world he saw brought him great fame.

Possessed of tremendous physical energy, he would spend hours walking and learning about his beloved countryside, climbing to the tops of hills to watch clouds, the sky, the flowers and his descriptions are a joy to read.

Richard Jefferies was also a lover of the sea and he died at the early age of thirty-eight in Sussex.

The house in which he was born at Coate, near Swindon, is now a museum to his memory. It is marked by a tablet, and the five rooms are filled with a variety of fascinating things — musical instruments from all over the world, relics from Pompeii, old china, one of the best collection of shells in existence, Wiltshire pictures, metals and minerals — and, last but not least, one of the biggest crocodiles in England!

I think Richard Jefferies would have been delighted that Coate Water is now a leisure centre where a variety of rural pursuits can be enjoyed.

JOHN OF SALISBURY

John, whose real name was Little, was born at Old Sarum between 1115 and 1120. He was proud of his birthplace and his family, and a fellow pupil with Thomas a Becket.

He came to Canterbury as Clerk and was appointed secretary to Archbishop Theobald, retaining his post when Becket succeeded as Primate.

John was a devoted and loyal follower of Becket and narrowly escaped a similar fate when the great Archbishop was murdered. During the turbulent years of Becket's Primacy, John had shared his exile, but was always said to have been eager to return to England, the more particularly to see his aged mother.

In 1176 John was appointed Bishop of Chartres where he died in 1180, leaving behind a treasure house of his writings.

SARAH JONES

This remarkable old lady was buried in St Bartholomew's churchyard at Corsham in 1753, at the age of one hundred and seven.

Her tombstone reads:

"Sometime before her death, she had fresh teeth."

JOUSTING

The first tournament held in England was claimed to have taken place at Salisbury in 1194 in the reign of Richard I.

In the Middle Ages tournaments were very popular events and often accompanied by a "fayre" at which local products were sold. The crowds were also entertained by jesters and wrestlers.

Richard I, needing money for his Crusades and the cost of the wars with France, created the first system of licensed tourneying. On the 22nd August 1194, the king wrote to the Archbishop of Canterbury requesting him to license jousts in England. A licence fee of 20 marks was payable for an earl; 10 marks for a baron and either 4 or 2 marks for a knight, depending on whether he held land. To collect this tax, the king limited his tournaments to five specified places, Salisbury being one of them.

JUBILEE FESTIVAL, 1893

The month of July 1893 was a special one for Marlborough College as it marked the Jubilee Celebrations of fifty years of the great public school founded in 1843 for the sons of the Clergy on the Marlborough Downs.

The town itself joined in with a will, and many buildings were gaily decorated with flags hung from houses in the High Street. At night, there were illuminations.

The College festivities included the traditional Field Day with the College Corps, spick and span, on parade for a visiting General; Old Marlburians' Dinner when some 500 sat down together and celebrated. Amongst the august company the roll included two VCs — Admiral Sir Nowell Salmon and Sir Evelyn Wood representing the Army — surely a proud achievement in so short a time.

Special Services were held in the Chapel, a Cricket Match — the School versus Old Captains, a Concert and a Boys' Supper and Prize Day.

At the Boys' Supper when, with the Master, present Marlburians celebrated, speeches were greeted by spontaneous bursts of applause, accompanied by the waving of handkerchiefs. This "gratuitous advertisement of the College Laundry continued throughout the evening."

THE KENNET AND AVON CANAL

England, in the nineteenth century, was gripped by canal fever, and Wiltshire was no exception.

The Kennet and Avon canal, which almost cuts the county in half, was the work of John Rennie, and the Act of Parliament authorising its construction was passed in 1794. It connects the River Kennet at Newbury in Berkshire to the Avon in Somerset, and in its heyday, barges containing grain, stone and timber were seen on its waters.

At Devizes, the builder sited some twenty-nine locks which rise in a marvellous staircase of engineering wonder.

The rise of the railways caused a decline in canal traffic and it is no longer used for the passage of goods. Unfortunately, it fell into decay and, but for the indefatigable work of the Trust, would still be choked with weeds and debris. Happily their work has restored stretches of the canal and pleasure boats journey in a leisurely manner on summer days along its grassy banks.

The Devizes to Westminster Canoe Race, initiated in 1948, by four members of the Devizes Rover Scouts, takes place annually on Good Friday. The course is some 125 miles from Devizes wharf to Westminster Bridge, and includes the negotiation of 77 locks. Often described as one of the toughest sporting events, the race now attracts 200 crews each year.

The builders of this waterway must be pleased that their work is still usable and enjoyed by many to this day.

A KING IN HIGH BOOTS

The north gate of the Cathedral Close at Salisbury was originally built as part of the fortifications by Bishop de Mortival in 1327, and was granted a licence from Edward III for this purpose. This side of the magnificent gate is embellished by a Royal Coat of Arms.

It is perhaps appropriate that the south side bears a statue of Edward VII to commemorate his visit to the City. The unusual feature of this small statue is that, it would seem the King, though suitably robed, appears to be wearing high boots. A statue of King Charles, wearing high boots, once stood on this site, but was destroyed by the Roundheads in the Civil War, and Edward VII has "stepped into his shoes."

LABOUR IN VAIN INN

Many years ago, at Cherhill, there was an Inn called the "Labour in Vain".

It gained this name from its sign which depicted a European maid trying to wash an Ethiopian baby white in a large tub! Unfortunately, all trade disappeared and the inn fell into disuse, but it is not forgotten.

LACOCK

A beautiful example of old England, Lacock is without doubt, one of Wiltshire's most picturesque villages.

The village was already established when Ela, Countess of Salisbury and widow of William Longespee, founded an abbey for Augustine nuns in 1232. The village itself was prosperous for the wool trade flourished here which explains the somewhat unusual width of some of the cottages.

After the Dissolution of the Monasteries, the Abbey came into the possession of the Talbot family in the sixteenth century. One of its most famous sons was William Henry Fox Talbot the photographic pioneer.

Many of the buildings are medieval in design and there is a friendly informality about them, representing every century from the thirteenth. One, by the shop of the National Trust who own the village, has the unusual feature of a clock let into the door.

The Church of St Cyriac is particularly famous for its stained glass and heraldic work, and one of the memorials includes a funeral hatchment. A fifteenth century brass depicts a whole family including eighteen children and two dogs.

The George Inn, one of the oldest continuously licensed inns in the country, dates from 1361, and has a seventeenth century dog spit.

The packhorse bridge is in one of the most charming parts of the village, and in medieval times was busy with pannier-laden ponies taking the goods for sale.

Once, the village was self-sufficient with its own shops, and even a brewery, but though life in the twentieth century has quickened the pace, it retains its charm. Nothing can surely change the gentle manner of this place which once knew the swish of nuns' habits as they went about their work in the Abbey and village.

THE LADIES OF IDMISTON

Idmiston is a delightful little village in the Bourne Valley surrounded by hills.

The church, which is part twelfth century contains a series of female faces carved into the stone corbels which carry the roof timbers. A charming addition, they are known as "The Ladies of Idmiston" and are surrounded by carvings of handsome men and angels playing instruments or carrying shields.

THE LANSDOWNE MONUMENT

Towering majestically above the town of Calne on the Cherhill Downs, the Lansdowne Monument is one of the most conspicuous landmarks in the county.

This column, which rises some one hundred and twenty-five feet high, can be seen — on a clear day — for some thirty miles. It was erected on the instructions of the Third Marquis of Lansdowne, who had a passion for such edifices, in memory of his ancestor, Sir William Petty, of the seventeeenth century.

The contract, dated 1845, showed that Charles Barry was the designer, for which he received £92, and Daniel and Jones of Bradford-on-Avon were the actual builders at a cost of £1,359. This was a huge sum for the nineteenth century particularly for a memorial which was later abandoned.

The Marquis had second thoughts about the memorial to his ancestor, thinking it more appropriate that he should be remembered in the graveyard of the Abbey Church at Romsey where he was buried.

So this column which is unmarked by any inscription — only a notice "This monument is dangerous" — became known as the Lansdowne Monument, which was perhaps the original intention of its creator!

LARDY CAKE

This is a very well-known Wiltshire cake and sometimes called "Shaley Cake" by older people. It was usually served hot, for tea at weekends.

Ingredients :

1 lb of white bread dough
Lard
Granulated sugar
Mixed spice (optional)

Roll the dough on a floured pastry-board. Put dabs of lard all over it, about the size of a walnut and about 1½ ins apart. Sprinkle with the sugar. Fold into three from the ends, and then into three from the sides. Turn to the right and roll out again. Repeat twice, each time putting on dabs of lard. After three such foldings and lardings, roll out to size of baking-tin, score across with a knife. Bake in a moderate oven. If preferred, add mixed spice, currants or sultanas to the mixture.

THE LAST WILD BOAR

In 1629, Sir Richard Grobham was Steward of Longford Castle and he lived at Wishford Manor in the reign of Elizabeth I. An enthusiastic hunter, he was particularly remembered by the villagers because he slew a large wild boar — for long the terror of the neighbourhood. His sword and helmet were hung in the church to commemorate the event, and Sir Richard's tomb is one of Wiltshire's finest seventeenth century monuments. Under the canopy Sir Richard lies in gold and white armour with scarlet strappings his feet (appropriately-) resting on a gilded boar's head carved in wood.

The story goes that Sir Richard chased this fearsome boar until he cornered the animal under a tree and wounded it — ever since, the tree has been known as "The Boar's Tree". Mortally wounded, the boar managed to swim across the River Wylye and died on the far bank.

Sir Richard was believed to have been the last man to kill a wild boar in Groveley Forest.

HENRY LAWES

This distinguished musician was born in the parish of Dinton on New Year's Day, 1595 and quickly established himself.

His father, Thomas Lawes, was a Vicar-choral in Salisbury Cathedral which produced many able singers and musicians in its day, and Henry Lawes was no exception.

As a celebrated composer and performer, he was appointed to be one of the private musicians to King Charles I. During the Commonwealth. he supported himself by teaching music. Many poets, including

Milton, admired his genius and were anxious to have their works set to his music.

Two years before his death in 1662, he composed the anthem sung at the coronation of King Charles II.

A LEG IS INTERRED HERE

Once, near Devizes, (according to an eighteenth century periodical) there stood an ancient wooden monument bearing the following inscription:

A Leg Is Interred Here

The writer moralises in the following strain —

A leg alone within a grave!
Graver I fear thou'rt some arch knave
Or else some dull poetic noddy
Pray, had this leg nor head nor body?

LINK WITH SOUTH AFRICA

During the Boer War, men of the Wiltshire Regiment carved out a chalk horse on the slopes of Naval Hill overlooking the city of Bloemfontein, the judicial capital of the republic of South Africa. Maybe it was nostalgia for their native county with its white horses that made them leave a lasting memorial in a foreign land.

THE LIONESS OF WINTERSLOW

In October 1816 the Pheasant Inn at Winterslow, at that time known as the Winterslow Hut, was the scene of a dramatic and exciting occurrence.

A travelling menagerie parked in the forecourt of the Inn, and as the Exeter Mail Coach drew up, one of the leading horses was pounced upon by a lioness. She had escaped from the menagerie and none of her keepers had noticed her disappearance. Panic ensued — the passengers from the coach ran into the inn and bolted and barred the door. The coachman and the guard, probably too scared to move — remained on their high seats, though in fairness, the guard did try to shoot the lion with his blunderbuss. A gallant Newfoundland dog grabbed the lioness by a leg but was driven back by the fierce claws, badly mauled by the attempt. The dog's attack distracted the lioness from her prey and she hid among the staddle stones supporting the granary.

By this time, the menagerie owner and his assistants, fearing to lose so valuable an animal, showed remarkable courage by crawling under the granary. By the light of candles, they placed a sack near the lion, forced her to lie on it, then secured her four legs and her mouth. They pulled her from her hiding place and, with the aid of six strong men, she was carried into her den in the caravan and secured.

The poor horse whose name was Pomegranate, was on show with all her wounds, at Salisbury Fair the next day.

One of the passengers was so terrified when the lioness brushed against him in his wild rush for the door that he went mad!

LITTLECOTE

This mellowed Tudor brick and stone Manor House was built between 1490 and 1520 and was the home of the Darrells.

With its long history it is one of the most interesting houses in the county, for spanning the centuries, it has known family life, tragedy, murder and occupation.

Perhaps its most famous owner was William or "Wild" Darrell who was accused of the murder of an infant and died violently after his acquittal. He is said to haunt his old home to this day.

Many august persons have lived here, one of them Sir John Popham, Lord Chief Justice of England whose family held the property until 1922.

In a house with perhaps more than its share of treasure, the Great Hall has true magnificence, measuring some forty-six feet by twenty-four feet, and twenty-five feet high. It is panelled all round, with an English, simply moulded ceiling and floor of grey and white flagstones.

History relates that Henry VIII brought Jane Seymour to this house, and one of the south windows bears their initials.

During the Civil War, Colonel Alexander Popham was a Roundhead, and his officers and men were garrisoned at the house. The buff uniform coats and armour hanging on the walls are unique. To his credit, Colonel Popham was later one of the officers who aided General Monk to restore Charles II to his throne, and the King dined in the house in 1663 after pardoning the owner. Colonel Popham left another memento — a Shovel Board Table, thirty feet long and believed the longest of its kind. The playing discs, bearing his initials, are still in a container fixed to the end of the table.

The Dutch parlour is so called as its walls carry paintings by Dutch prisoners of war, but perhaps its most unique feature is the Cromwellian Chapel, believed to be the only example of such a Chapel in existence, it has no altar but an elevated pulpit stands in its place. This simple, plain Chapel has an air of peace and unvarnished, real worship within its walls.

The list is endless — William of Orange stayed here and there is a haunted landing and bedroom (where the child was murdered), of course, Queen Elizabeth I's bedroom, and a Jerusalem Staircase, the oldest in the house which is haunted, and on the sunniest day, a place to chill.

There is more, much more, and Littlecote possesses the quality of tenacity that lures its visitors to return another day, once more to savour its delights.

LONG BARROW, WEST KENNETT

The largest monument of its kind in Britain, the Long Barrow has attracted hundreds of visitors since it was partly excavated in 1859 and again a century later.

A huge tomb it is covered by a coffin-shaped mound some three hundred and thirty feet long and eighty feet wide, it was dated about 2.500 BC.

One of the finest Neolithic long barrows in this country, it possesses a long passage and five burial chambers and the pillars and capstones were of sarsen stone.

Excavations revealed that at least forty-six people had been buried — men, women and children and some infants. Pottery was found among the grave goods contained in the tomb which suggested the dead had been people of the Beaker period, and the tomb had been in use for more than a thousand years, possibly by the ruling families. It would seem, from the great care taken in its preparation that the burial chamber was a very special place to which sacred pilgrimages were made. There is evidence of religious ceremonies having taken place on the site.

Local legend claims that at sunrise on the longest day of the year, the tomb is entered by a priest who is followed by a huge, white hound with red ears.

LONGEVITY

Possibly due to the pure air of the county, or maybe, just clean living, Wiltshire people are known for their longevity.

It is recorded that three ladies — Elizabeth Goulding, Grace Young and Elizabeth Wiltshire, whose combined ages totalled just three hundred years, were all buried the same day in 1695 at Bremhill.

LONGLEAT

For its size, Wiltshire has been rich in pioneers of all kinds, so it is not surprising that the Sixth Marquess of Bath was the first Peer to open his home regularly to visitors, twenty-seven years ago. Since then, many others have followed suit, but it was a Wiltshire home that blazed the Stately Home trail.

The home of the Thynne family for over four hundred years, Longleat, like many other great English houses, was at first a monastic establishment. In the valley watered by a stream — the Long Leat — Augustinian Canons built a priory in the thirteenth century, and when Henry VIII dissolved the monasteries, it passed to the Crown and in 1540 was sold for £53 to Sir John Thynne.

Much restoration and building work has taken place but it is today one of the finest examples of the Italianate architecture of Elizabeth I's reign, and in the eighteenth century the park was landscaped by Capability Brown for the third Viscount Weymouth who became the first Marquess of Bath in 1789.

The Great Hall, which was carefully planned by Sir John Thynne in 1559, with stone-flagged floor and hammer-beam support, remains unchanged today, except for the fireplace and Minstrels' Gallery added in 1600 and a small balcony.

The State Dining Room has been the scene of many banquets for visiting royalty from Queen Elizabeth I who was an interested spectator, coming while the building work was still in progress. On one wall hangs a portrait of Maria Audley, first wife of Sir Thomas Thynne, the third owner and grandson of the builder. Convinced by a dream that she would die in childbirth, she asked that her portrait be painted — and the dream came true.

The family State Coach, built in 1750, has been used at every coronation since that of George IV in 1821. Sir Christopher Wren designed a Grand Staircase which was removed in 1808 at the suggestion of Wyatt. During this work, coffins containing skeletons of some of the Black Canons were found and buried in nearby Horningsham churchyard. It was Wyatt who built the stables which are so designed as to seem part of the original house.

The gardens, with the Orangery and Rose Gardens are a delight and there is a charming Pets' Cemetery showing that the family animals were never to be forgotten.

Longleat has served its country in two world wars. In the 1914 War the house was used as a convalescent home for the wounded, and in the Second World War provided a refuge for a Girls' School from Bath whose buildings were requisitioned by the Admirality.

In opening his home to the public the present Marquess has shown the spirit of service common to his ancestors in sharing a magnificent inheritance with everyday people. Today, though the great house in its almost perfect setting, remains part of the unchanging scene, the advent of the world-known Safari Park with lions, tigers and giraffes roaming freely in the grounds is a source of pleasure to those who prefer outdoor excitement.

MALMESBURY

Famous for over a thousand years, this ancient market town stands high on a hill between the River Avon and its tributary, the Inglebourne, and the town, except for the northwest, is completely surrounded by water.

It owes its origin to the great Abbey which goes back to the seventh century, and one of England's famous Kings, the first to unite all England, Athelstan, grandson of the great Alfred, lies buried there.

Dunstan, Archbishop of Canterbury presented the Abbey with an organ, the first known in Britain.

Nowadays, a huge fragment of the abbey church stands, with the Norman nave serving as the parish church. The nave, dated 1168, is large enough to give some idea of the size of the whole building which is enhanced by many sculptures and paintings, one reputedly by a pupil of Michelangelo. The Monks of Malmesbury wrote four immense volumes of the Bible which are among the treasures.

Another of Wiltshire's weaver towns, Malmesbury has retained many of its attractive grey stone buildings and the cottage-lined streets lead to the market cross, which octagonal and roofed, is a superb example of sixteenth century stonemasonry.

William the Conquerer endowed the Abbey and Edward the Confessor showered gifts upon it, and its roll includes William of Malmesbury who was one of its scholars.

Naturally, there is a ghost, and the Abbey grounds are said to be haunted by the ghost of a grey lady who disappears into a hedge — the place never growing.

THE MAN IN THE CELLAR

It is said that the Green Lady's Walk at Longleat House is haunted by Lady Louise Carteret who was the wife of the second Viscount Weymouth.

She had a lover, and when her husband found out, he killed the unfortunate man in a duel and buried him beneath the cellar floor. This was in the eighteenth century, and since that time, Lady Carteret has been seen pacing disconsolately along the corridors.

When central heating was being installed the remains of a young man, wearing the clothes of the period of the murder, was found beneath the cellar floor.

THE MARKET TOWN IN THE CENTRE

Devizes, one of the old market towns in the county is proud of its heritage and jealous of its reputation.

In the eleventh century, its Castle, built there by Bishop Roger, was said to be the finest in Europe, but was destroyed by Roundhead troops in the Civil War, as the area was the scene of a fierce battle won by the Royalists. Now a private house, the castle still bears traces of its original glory in the fine arch of its entrance.

Dominating the scene is, of course, the Market Place — a wide, fine square of differing buildings and a long, long history. This place has seen the famous and the infamous come and go, witnessed the amazing incident of the market woman who dropped dead after telling a lie and known glory and tragedy. Naturally, as a market town, this area is the focal point and the houses that surround the famous square jostle happily in a blend of old and new. The Bear Hotel, once the home of Thomas Lawrence the painter still looks as it must have done in his day, as probably does the Black Swan which is dated 1737.

The town has its share of fine houses, with an Elizabethan alley of timbered houses nestling behind a busy street, and Long Street which provides a Norman parish church, has a fine collection of Georgian houses climbing its gentle slopes.

This ancient town boasts some three hundred "listed" buildings, among them the Queen Anne delight, Brownston House, with nearby fifteenth century Great Porch House well preserved.

Within recent memory, the town had a flourishing Snuff factory which is still remembered by a street name, and other curious names include the Brittox from the French for "defences" being once a stockaded area, and Nursteed which is "where the nuts are grown".

Devizes seems typically Wiltshire, maintaining a sturdy independence so common to the county, and a contentment with its achievement. It has a long and proud history and has survived its tribulations. One has the feeling that it always will.

MARLBOROUGH COLLEGE

In August 1843, the first gathering of 200 boys in the halls of the Seymours at Marlborough was an unprecedented event.

The initiative in the movement to found Marlborough College belongs to the Reverend Charles Plater whose scheme it was in 1842.

Marlborough was originally founded for the sons of clergy and developed later into one of the most famous boys' public schools in England.

The main aim was to give a "first class education at a low price" for the sons of clergymen. At this time, most of the other great public schools were beyond the means of most parsons. Two thirds of the boys were sons of the clergy and the remaining third of laymen. The former paid 30 guineas per year, the latter 50 guineas, and admission was by nomination of Governors and Life Governors who themselves paid for the privilege.

Two hundred boys took their places the first day, and in five years, the school was second to Eton numerically. At first, it was said Marlborough was the most successful of all the great schools.

Its rural setting of "open downs, so rich in monuments" and the vastness of Savernake Forest on its doorstep are unequalled and a great heritage for any school.

As time passed, Marlborough grew and made its own traditions, its own slang and survived the vicissitudes that beset most schools in the nineteenth century. But it survived.

Two wars brought high honours to its OMs who served their country, and a sadness for those who would never return. The Memorial Hall, built in 1923, is a reminder of their sacrifice.

Nearly one hundred and fifty years later Marlborough is still a great school with a fine tradition.

There is an atmosphere that is special to the School — a certain pride, accepted with seeming indifference. In all, there is a tenaciousness about Marlborough that calls to its sons from the far corners of the earth. In wars, they were distinguished, in peace they have taken their place in shaping the destiny of the world, and all remember their schooldays in rural Wiltshire. It is strange that the school stretches its influence for a wide area, and OMs flock to walk again in Court or sit, leisurely, beside the cricket field on Prize Day. And it is known that it would be unthinkable for the son of an Old Marlburian to go to another school.

It is difficult for me to think of Marlborough without nostalgia, for — it seems another decade now — I worked there for three years. One of my most vivid memories is of Morning Service in Chapel with nearly a thousand voices raised in praise of God, and the sunlight glinting on the tall candlesticks flanking the altar. I never pass along the Bath Road without memory stirring — the boys I knew have gone, but like eternity, Marlborough has a continuity and seems timeless — to me.

MARLBOROUGH SHEEP - FAIR DAY "SOUP"

Ingredients:

½ lb lean mutton or lamb
(from neck, shoulder or leg)
1 or 2 onions, or handful of
spring onions, using green
2 cups of peas
1 cupful shredded lettuce
1 cupful water
Salt and pepper

Cut the meat into small pieces. Put in pan with peas, sliced onion and lettuce, add water and salt and pepper. Bring to boil and cook very gently until the meat is tender — about an hour. Add extra, rich stock but do not make too liquid. Turn into hot dish or tureen and serve with new potatoes, home-made bread or rice.

(*This was an economical and useful dish often used when the sheepkeeping community flourished on the Marlborough Downs*).

MEMORIAL TO MARY STIFF

There is a grave at Highworth to the memory of Mary Stiff who died there, in 1714, at the age of 107. Stiff indeed!

MILDENHALL

Mildenhall is a typical, brick village with thatched cottages, tile and slate houses and known locally as "Minall".

The Church of St John the Baptist was described by Sir John Betjeman as a "country church which neither Victorians nor our own generation has touched."

The little church is one for the imaginative, for closing one's eyes and, then opening them, you may see in your mind's eye, a place filled with worshippers from a Jane Austen novel.

The high box pews — so high that only the heads of the men and women are visible, are lined with baize in red, green or blue, painted white on the outside.

The squire's pew is special. It is larger than the rest in a special aisle to itself, and years ago, was the family chapel where mass was said for the souls of his ancestors. It even has its own fireplace and there are miniature benches for the children.

Medieval paintings of saints and devils hang on the walls with a Royal Arms of George III over the chancel arch. Two huge, three-decker pulpits, one with a sounding board above, are approached by a flight of steps. An hour-glass in an iron stand is by the pulpit desk, and below, yet another pulpit from which the parson reads the prayers and lessons before climbing upwards for his sermon.

And there is a third pulpit for the parish clerk to sit and call "Amen".

Mildenhall possesses one of the few remaining churches that contain, unchanged, their Georgian fittings. If one closes one's eyes and listens to the service, it is easy to imagine oneself in another, long forgotten and leisurely world.

Plate 1—Marlborough Downs.

Plate 3—Tithe Barn, Bradford on Avon.
Plate 2—Bradford on Avon Bridge.

Plate 4—Salisbury Cathedral.

Plate 5—A Dewpond.
Plate 6—Thatch Hooks, West Lavington.

Plate 7—Bishop's Cannings Church.

Plate 8—Meditation Chair.

Plate 9—Salisbury Plain.

Plate 10—Wootton Rivers Church.

Plate 11—Obelisk, St John's churchyard, Devizes.

Plate 12—Stonehenge.

Plate 13—Robbers' Stone.

Plate 14—Steeple Ashton.

Plate 15—Urchfont.

Plate 16—West Kennett Longbarrow.

Plate 17—Silbury Hill.

Plate 18—Lacock Abbey.

Plate 19—Maud Heath Monument.

Plate 20—Castle Combe.
Plate 21—Aldbourne.

Plate 22 Porch House, Potterne.

Plate 23—Tithe Barn, Tisbury.
Plate 24—Marlborough High Street.

Plate 25—Devizes Market Cross.
Plate 26—Market Place, Devizes.

MILESTONES

The Salisbury area is rich in old milestones, many of them showing distances to "Sarum" and "Shaston".

For instance, on the old Turnpike Road on Fovant Down there is a stone dating back to 1756, and the road to East Knoyle has very old stones which also show the parish name.

Near West Amesbury is a large stone, dated 1764, showing the miles from London and Andover in Roman numerals, and others on major (and minor) roads also give distances from Hyde Park Corner.

Another feature of Wiltshire's roads are the old hand pumps still to be seen by the side of the road and much welcomed by coach travellers in days gone by. There is a fine specimen at Potterne, just out of the village, on the way to Lavington.

MILITARY MANOEUVRES

Though Salisbury Plain has long been famed as an ideal area for military training, the largest military manoeuvres the county has ever known took place at Alderbury in September 1910.

A large house party, which included the Duke of Connaught, Sir Winston Churchill, Lord Kitchener and Lord Roberts, had gathered at the country home, Wilton House, of Lord Pembroke for the occasion, and they turned out in force — with their ladies to see the excitement.

Some forty-eight thousand troops were involved, divided into opposing armies for the battle on the Plain, superintended by Sir John French.

The airship *Beta* was used for military reconnaissance in this operation, the first time an airship was ever used in this way.

Unfortunately, it was forced down with a burst carburettor, but not before it had made military history.

MIRACLE PLACE

Set in the heart of the lovely Wylye valley, with a river flowing through it, the attractive village of Bishopstrow is a miracle place.

As its name implies, it was once connected with a Bishop. And, who else, but St Aldhelm.

Legend recalls that the Saint was walking here and planted his staff in the ground where it miraculously changed into an ash tree, and the place became known as "Bishop's Treow" or the "'Bishop's Tree."

Long historical associations have centred round this beautiful place for the Romans built a house here and the Saxons a church, but neither remain. Alfred camped here after his defeat by the Danes, and eight hundred years later, Cromwell breakfasted under a yew tree here after the Battle of Newbury.

THE MONK IN THE LIBRARY

The village of Avebury is rich in history and its Elizabethan Manor House is no exception. It was built in the sixteenth century and stands on the site of a priory of Benedictine monks, founded in 1110.

A maidservant saw a monk sitting in the library one day and asked her master if he was remaining to lunch — but he had disappeared. He must have wanted "food for thought"!

MOP FAIRS

For centuries, the autumn was the special season for fairs, for the farmer's harvest was gathered in, and it often provided a last chance for merry-making before the onset of winter.

Hiring fairs, as these celebrations were called, were held at various towns in Wiltshire, but Marlborough's Mop fairs are the best known and attended.

Servants were usually hired for a year, from Michaelmas to Michaelmas, and would line up according to their skills, wearing a token of their calling. Cowmen would sport a tuft of cowhair; shepherds sheepwool, a carter whipcord and so on. Maids carried a mop or wore a white apron, and the name Mop Fair was established.

Most Mop Fairs were held on market days, with a second a week or so later which gave a second chance for those still unemployed, or for masters to make a change if the servant was unsuitable.

Tradition for maidservants laid down that, on Mothering Sunday the following year, they would return home to their mothers and present them with the popular Simnel Cake.

When a servant was hired, he or she would put a ribbon in their hats to replace the token of their skills. These ribbons were bought by the employers to seal the bargain. Then the rest of the day was spent in merrymaking.

Marlborough still has its Mop Fairs which take place annually in October. Little Mop is on the Saturday nearest in date to the 11th October, and Big Mop a week later. Today, you will not see workers for hire, but the world of entertainment takes over, and the broad High Street is closed to traffic for the duration of the celebrations.

THE MORAVIANS

The Moravians who came to the little village of East Tytherton, in 1742, built a Georgian church there in 1792.

These "Bohemian Brothers" originated in 1457 among some of the followers of John Huess. They rejected the use of force, refused to take oaths and had no hierarchy, and were much persecuted.

In the eighteenth century they re-established themselves, and a "Sisters' House" for the training of women and girls "wanting to improve their education or be employed in needlework" was opened in Tytherton. It closed in 1880.

In the graveyard, leaves drift silently across the very simple, almost severe tombs of these people — recording no more than name, date of death and age.

MUSHROOM MINING

Sixty years ago, before the outbreak of the First World War, a French family settled in Bradford-on-Avon and brought to the town a new and unusual industry which still flourishes today.

With characteristic foresight and ingenuity, the Baumann family realised the potential of some disused limestone quarries, and took full advantage of the light and air conditions prevailing. These proved perfect for mushroom growing and the industry grew.

For seven days a week, three hundred and sixty four days a year (the factory closes only on Christmas Day) the mushrooms are carefully tended by workers who spend their time underground wearing lights attached to their heads (like coal miners) carefully selecting from the tiered trays.

Manure for the specially prepared compost comes from racing stables all over the country.

NASTURTIUM SAUCE

Ingredients:

1 quart pressed nasturtium flowers
1 quart vinegar
8 shallots (bruised)
6 cloves
1 teaspoon salt
Small pinch Indian soy
½ level teaspoon cayenne pepper

Simmer all except the flowers together for 10 minutes, then pour over the flowers. Cover closely for two months. Strain and pour into bottles, adding a little Indian soy before corking securely.

(*This is an old country recipe*).

A LINK WITH NELSON

Pewsey is an old town and its ancient church stands on sarsen stones, probably laid by the Saxons, so it is fitting that a large statue of King Alfred should stand sentinel at the crossroads.

The fine church, with many features, has altar rails made from the timbers of the *San Josef* captured by Admiral Lord Nelson in 1797. The lock of the almsbox has a sad origin — it came from the door of a convict cell in Van Diemen's Land.

That is not all that is old in Pewsey. It possesses a cruck-built, medieval gabled and half-timbered house. The main timbers of cruck-built gables were a curving oak tree split down the centre and up-ended so that the tips met and locked in position to carry the ridge poles, braced by oak beams laid across them and massively pegged. These crucks were often the lowlier dwellings of peasants, and this one at Pewsey is rare and impressive; a fine example of the few remaining in England.

Pewsey has a modern side too. In September every year it stages a Carnival and is said to have been the "mother of all West Country Carnivals". I wonder if Alfred approves?

WIILTSHIRE'S FIRST NEWSPAPER

Steeple Ashton church possesses a palimpsest brass which hangs on the north wall.

One side bears a tribute to Deborah Marks who died in 1750 at the ripe old age of 99, after living under Cromwell and seven kings and queens of England.

The reverse shows a picture of a stout figure of Queen Anne standing with upraised sword by a scale in which is a Bible, her crowned consort and two Bishops. A roughly drawn church, labelled "The Church of England" forms the background and a small cowled figure is running away from the group, saying 'Burn the heretic book' and other remarks.

A verse below shows that the brass was a vigorous Protestant attack on Roman Catholicism in the days of Queen Anne.

The brass was engraved by Samuel Farley who produced Wiltshire's first newspaper, printing it himself. Published in 1715, the paper was entitled *The Salisbury Postman.*

OLD SARUM

This pre-history site a few miles from the City of Salisbury covers an area of some fifty-six acres on which stood an Iron Age Camp, and later the Romans, Saxons and Danes encamped there.

William the Conqueror reviewed his troops there in 1070. A Castle and Cathedral were built in the eleventh century, but disagreements between the soldiers and the clergy caused it to fall into ruin. The new Cathedral in the City of Salisbury was built to replace it.

The name has never been forgotten and though the town there declined in the thirteenth century the hill was represented in Parliament until 1852! One of Sarum's Members of Parliament was William Pitt, Lord Chatham, who was Prime Minister — a fine politician but one with an uninhabited constituency.

OLDEST CLOCK IN WILTSHIRE

Stonehenge is claimed to be the oldest clock in Wiltshire, or perhaps the whole country. It tells the time of *year* rather than the time of day.

OLD SOLDIER BREMHILL

The tomb of an old soldier at Bremhill reads:

On an old Soldier, aged 92
A poor old soldier shall not lie unknown,
Without a verse and this recording stone.
'Twas his, in youth, o'er distant lands to stray,
Danger and death companions of his way.
Here, in his native village, stealing age
Closed the long evenings of his pilgrimage.
Speak of the past — of names of high renown,
Or brave commanders long to dust gone down,
His look with instant animation glow'd,
Tho' ninety winters on his head had snow'd
His country, while he lived, a boon supplied,
And Faith, her shield held o'er him when he died.

OLIVER THE MONK

For centuries, men have attempted to imitate bird's flight and very seldom with success.

One Wiltshireman who tried it was a monk called Oliver from Malmesbury. In 1010, he made himself a pair of wings and attempted to fly from the top of the tower of Malmesbury Abbey. He fell to the ground and was fortunate to escape death, though he was crippled for life.

In 1066, on seeing Halley's Comet, he is said to have prophesied the Norman Conquest and consequent disaster for England.

LADY O'LOONEY

An epitaph in Pewsey Churchyard reads:

Here lies the body of Lady O'Looney
Great niece of Burke
Commonly called the Sublime
She was
Bland, passionate and deeply religious
Also, she painted in water colours,
And sent several pictures
to the exhibition.
She was first cousin
to Lady Jones
and of such
is the Kingdom of Heaven.

ONE OF THE SMALLEST

Standing in a field on a grassy hill, is the tiny church of St Martin's at Fifield Bavant, a pretty village in the Chalk Valley.

Measuring only thirty-five feet in length and fifteen feet in width, this is said to be one of the smallest churches in England. Its roof beams are dark with age and the font is Norman, from whom the name originated. Fifield represents the five fields or hides of land and the Bavant comes from the Norman owners.

OPEN AIR MUSEUM

Surely, only Wiltshire could possess a Museum of Gravestones! In the village of Great Bedwyn, in the main street, one can see an unusual sight, for ranged against a wall. outside the monumental masons, are an amazing number of headstones.

Here are displayed memorials to tradesmen, clergymen, some humorous, some sad, and even pets are remembered.

A smith is remembered thus:

My sledge and hammer lie reclined
My bellows they have lost their wind
My fire is extinct — my forge decayed
And in the dust my vice is layed.
My coal is spent — my iron is gone
My nails are driven — my work is done.
My fire-dried corpse lies here at rest
My soul well smoked soars to be blest.

Very often the epitaphs contained warnings — but for the Grace of God — and sly jokes, and in these times when few memorials are placed in churchyards unless they are factual, it is interesting to realise that our ancestors could often joke about the great beyond.

A small Terrier, whose life was short, made his mark:

Very small and very bold
He always "died" when he was told.

So, Touser, at least will never be forgotten.

PATTENS

The path leading to St Mary's Church at Marlborough is known as Patten's Alley, for years ago, it was the place where women attending the Service left their pattens. The shelf provided for this purpose remained until a few years ago.

PATTY'S BOTTOM

The village of Woodmanton has a small valley known as Patty's Bottom. For some, this is a place of terror, for on certain nights, it is haunted by the sound of tramping footsteps, and the occasional appearance of galloping, *headless* horses.

Local tradition says that a terrible battle between the Romans and British was fought here, and so great was the carnage that the whole valley was filled with blood.

COLONEL JOHN PENRUDDOCK

In the tiny church of Compton Chamberlayne is a memorial to a very brave Englishman who lived in Compton Park in the time of the Commonwealth.

His name is immortalised in the only Royalist rising against the Government of Oliver Cromwell. Penruddock's Rising or the Wiltshire Rising as it is sometimes known, took place in March 1655.

Four hundred rebels, led by Colonel Penruddock, seized the City of Salisbury, freed the prisoners, arrested the Judges and Sheriff and proclaimed Charles II King in the Market Square.

Without waiting for the promised Hampshire reinforcements, Penruddock and his force marched westwards, hoping to raise the traditional Royalist support in the West Country.

At South Molton, however, they were attacked by a Roundhead force and, after a brief engagement on the 14th March, the Royalists broke up, Penruddock surrendered on quarter.

Taken to Exeter goal, Colonel Penruddock was beheaded, leaving a wife and seven children to mourn in their Wiltshire home.

The devotion of John Penruddock and his wife, Arundel, is a great love story, and a letter written to her husband while he was waiting death, shows his wife's outstanding fidelity.

This is the final paragraph:

"Adieu, therefore, ten thousand times my dearest dear, and since I must never see you more, take this prayer. 'May your faith be so strengthened, that constancy may continue, and then I hope heaven will receive you, where grief and love will in short time after, I hope, translate, my dear, your sad but constant wife, even to love your ashes when dead'."

The Penruddock family were connected with Compton Chamberlayne and its Park from 1398 until October 1946 when the last of the family was buried. A tablet commemorates their deeds, including the one who fought to restore his rightful king and two who gave their lives fighting in the First World War.

PIGS, PIGS, PIGS

Calne, a town whose history spans the centuries, was in its heyday when the great coaches rattled and bumped along the Wiltshire roads, and it was a favourite stopping place for travellers.

In the Middle Ages, it was another of the county's many weaving towns, but with the coming of machinery in the eighteenth century, the industry declined and Calne had to find another.

The fine pasturelands of the county had long been ideal for sheep and pigs, but it was the latter that brought real fame to this quiet, gentle place in 1770.

In that year a Sarah Harris opened a butcher's shop in Calne, ten years after the accession of George III. Gradually, the descendants of this enterprising woman built up the business adding bacon curing to their butchery and grocery.

One member of the family, George Harris, went to America and returned in the middle of the nineteenth century with an idea that was to revolutionise bacon curing. He built an icehouse in his High Street shop making it possible to cure bacon all the year round,

At that time, before the railway was constructed, large numbers of Irish pigs were driven in herds along the road from Bristol, through Calne and on London. This droving was a well organised service, with regular resting places, but the potato famine ruined the Irish trade.

The enterprise was saved by the introduction of the icehouse, and what in later years became world known, began.

Calne was now a "bacon" town and Wiltshire, like York, famed for its ham.

By 1900, an average of two thousand pigs were slaughtered each week and sausage making began in earnest, and the factory increased and prospered, being granted a royal warrant in 1929, an honour it has held ever since.

These days, the great premises of C and T Harris dominate the town, and its products travel the world where they are recognised and enjoyed.

Another Wiltshire firm had the same idea in 1778 when the firm of Bowyer was started by a miller, Abraham Bowyer. Now firmly established in Trowbridge, they too, ensure that Wiltshire is world renowned for its bacon.

RUTH PIERCE

Beware of falsehood! This might well be the epitaph of Ruth Pierce who was struck dead in Devizes market place in 1753, and this tragic event was duly recorded as an awful warning to others who might be tempted to lie.

A tablet describing her death hung in the market house, but when that house was demolished, Mr Halcombe of the Bear Inn, in order to keep the remembrance, displayed it on the base of a pillar supporting his sign in the market place. In 1801 the sign was taken down and the original tablet re-erected.

A memorial to Lord Sidmouth stands on one side of the Market Cross erected in 1814 at his expense, and one side records that it is a "memorial of his grateful attachment to the Borough of Devizes of which he has been Recorder thirty years and of which he was six times unanimously chosen a representative in Parliament".

The east side tells a different story.

"The Mayor and corporation of Devizes avail themselves of the stability of this building to transmit to future times the record of an awful event which occurred in this market place in the year 1753; hoping that such record may serve as a salutary warning against the danger of impiously invoking divine vengeance or of calling upon the Holy Name of God to conceal the devices of falsehood and fraud.

"On Thursday the 25 January 1753, Ruth Pierce of Potterne in the county, agreed with three other women to buy a sack of wheat in the market, each paying her due proportion towards the same; one of these women in collecting the several quotas of money, discovered a deficiency, and demanded of Ruth Pierce the sum which was wanting to make good the amount. Ruth Pierce protested that she had paid her share, and said, "She wished she might drop down dead if she had not.' She rashly repeated this awful wish, when, to the consternation and terror of the surrounding multitude, she instantly fell down and expired, having the money concealed in her hand."

It would surely be a rash person who emulated her claim in Devizes today.

THE PLAGUE

Seventeenth century England was much afflicted by plague and the quiet countryside of Wiltshire did not escape the dreaded scourge.

As a precaution, the Market at Salisbury was transferred to Wilton in 1627, and there is a stone between Harnham and Netherhampton called a "Plague Stone." This is the place where people left money in a basin of vinegar and the traders from Wilton left them their food.

In the little village of Urchfont, are two graves, said to be those of three brothers who died of plague. John, Jacob and Humphrey Giddons all perished in 1644, but only one grave is occupied. The third brother, having buried his two brothers in one grave, is said to have revived after "depositing himself" in the second grave.

PLUM SAUCE

Long ago, this was much favoured in Wiltshire to serve with lamb or mutton. It is made as follows: Stew one pound of stoned plums gently in ½ pint of white wine vinegar with 4 ozs sugar for about 10 minutes, or until soft. When ready, stir in a tablespoon of chopped, fresh mint. Serve hot.

POOR, BRAVE, PUSSY

A brave cat of fifteenth century Marlborough is remembered in carvings on the part Norman church of St Mary's which was reputed to have burnt down in 1460.

The story is that, when the church was burning, a cat had its kittens in the tower, and brought them out one by one, to safety, as the flames grew fiercer. However, on going back for the last one, the flames overcame her and she was burnt to death.

It is encouraging to think that not only human gallantry is remembered, and four hundred years later, this brave cat's action is not forgotten.

THE PORCH HOUSE, POTTERNE

The village of Potterne has many pleasant, attractive houses and is recorded in Domesday. Earlier, it was in the possession of the Bishops of Salisbury.

The Porch House, on the site of an ancient hostelry which once belonged to the Bishop of Salisbury, and was said to have been built for his steward, is a marvellously well-preserved example of an early Tudor dwelling.

Until the early part of this century, the house was known as Church House, presumably because it originally belonged to the Church, but has remained a freehold to the present day.

It was the home of the Pitt family for several generations until, in 1843, it passed to Henry Oliver, High Sheriff of Wiltshire. On his death, it was purchased by George Richmond, the portrait painter, who spent several years restoring the property — as far as possible — to its original beauty.

The house is what is termed a hall house of simple plan with a cross gabled office part, cross gabled solar part. During restoration work in 1872, some fifteenth century French coins were found, also a mummified chicken, possibly used as a foundation sacrifice.

The terraced gardens have a marble well head dated 1514 which came from Venice, and at the top of the garden is the site of the pre-conquest church of Potterne.

THE PREHISTORIC OX

Fishermen using a net in the deep pool in the Avon had a big surprise in May 1838 when, not far from the Vicarage field, they drew up a very heavy object. On examination it proved to be horns and part of the skull of an ox, and about a third larger than any they had seen before.

This remarkable discovery caused a stir in many pools and of a far wider area than Wiltshire. For it was proved that this was part of the fossil skull of a Prehistoric Ox and believed to have originated in the Palaeolithic era, and of a species extinct light years ago. The horns were more perfect, in the experts' view, than those found near Paris or the specimen in the British Museum.

Now, suitably mounted, the horns hang in pride of place over the door of the main hall in Melksham Town Hall.

PRESHUTE

This is an attractive little hamlet on the river above which stands the hill on which the boys from Mr Greazeley's School in Marlborough cut a white horse in 1804, the year before the Battle of Trafalgar. It is still there as a reminder of their efforts.

A short distance from Marlborough College itself and tucked away to itself is St George's fifteenth century church, with Norman arcades. There is a huge Norman font cut from a solid block of black marble, reputed to have come from Marlborough Castle. Legend claims that King John and his children were baptised in it.

A sad little sculpture shows two cherubs sobbing, with handkerchiefs to their eyes and a skull between them.

WILLIAM PRIOR

William Prior was a native of Devizes and promoted Lollardy in 1507.

For this crime, he was cited at Salisbury. He recanted. Then, he repented and resumed his former professions and was condemned and delivered to death by flames as a heretic.

THE PRIORY CHURCH OF EDINGTON

In 1352, William of Edington, Bishop of Winchester, but a native of the parish, founded a College for priests in the village. At the behest of the Black Prince this later became a monastery for the Augustinian Order of Bonshommes, friars of English origin who followed the Rule of the Augustines, and copied their dress.

Edington Priory is a perfect example of a small, monastic church of its age, and in some ways, resembles a Cathedral or even a fortified mansion on account of its curious battlements.

The inside is graceful with medieval tombs, some being salvaged from Imber church, and pride of place goes to the great screen, one of the few roodlofts remaining in England, though the roodbeam is missing.

There are a series of consecration crosses, with twelve inside and ten on outside walls, only two missing from the complete twenty-four. No church in England now has a complete set.

Although Edington has known great violence, for Bishop Ayscough was murdered there, now it enjoys a new tranquillity enhanced by its world-known musical festivals.

THE QUARRIES

To the south of the county, nestling in the beautiful Nadder Valley and with its own stream meandering quietly along, is the little village of Chilmark. It is a small place, yet world known because of the quantities of fine, creamy freestone quarried here, and used in so many of the county's stately homes and churches. Perhaps its greatest glory is that, though many of the priories built with the stone have vanished, the stone still stands in such wonders as Salisbury Cathedral which was constructed from it.

Since pre-Roman times the stone has been quarried here and the old quarries themselves are about the size of a cathedral.

John de Chilmark, a mathematician and philosopher of the fourteenth century, and called the "Archimedes of his age" was probably baptised in the church which still retains its seven hundred year old doorway.

In the 1600s, people from this parish took ship in the *Mayflower* for America where there is a place called Chilmark in Massachusetts where they settled.

THE RAILWAY TOWN

If ever a place could be said to have grown because of the railways, it is true of Swindon.

Though this is the largest, and highest, town in the county, for years it was little more than a village in the north where its pasture land was used successfully in dairy farming. There have been markets since 1274 and, in 1670, it was said that it "continued a gallant market for cattle."

As late as 1798, Swindon was a small place, nicknamed by some. "Swinedon" meaning a place for the keeping of pigs, and when writing letters, the people of Wroughton said their village was "near Marlborough" as a means of identification.

In 1840 everything changed. The railways came to Swindon, and legend recalls that the great engineer, Brunel, came to the town to decide on the best place for the railway. He is said to have had a picnic and thrown a sandwich, the point where it landed marking the site of the first building erected by the GWR.

The first line of three hundred cottages provided for railway workers were laid out on the south side by 1842, and later the railways made it "their town" by providing schools, a hospital and St Mark's Church, in 1845, for the railway workers.

In 1962 the town opened a railway museum retaining for posterity engines and other railway impedimenta that might be lost without it.

JOHN RATTLEBONE

One of the county's early heroes is John Rattlebone of Sherston where there are two memorials to his name. One is the name of the local inn — obviously, the Rattlebone — and the other is a little, carved figure near the south door of the church. It is alleged to be his likeness but this is probably untrue.

In 1016 Rattlebone is said to have fought a great battle against the Danes at a place named Sceorstan, said to be Sherston. The battle itself was indecisive but Rattlebone was badly injured in the stomach. Legend says that he seized a tile, holding it over the wound and fought on. He survived and was given the manor of Sherston as a reward for his bravery. There is an old song in the village which goes:

Fight well, Rattlebone,
Thou shalt have Sherston.

The Church contains a huge timber chest dating from the Middle Ages. According to local tradition, it was used to store Rathbone's armour and the initials "R.B." are carved on it.

RIOTS AND STRIFE

The year 1830 was a bad one for Wiltshire. A cold, wet summer had ruined the harvest and half-starving men reached the end of their patience. In bands, they roamed the countryside firing hay ricks and smashing agricultural machinery in frustration.

One man said, "We don't want to do mischief but we do want our poor children to go to bed with a full belly, instead of crying with half a belly full."

This was the great agricultural workers' revolt which affected Southern England. In Wiltshire, wages were particularly low, men earning about seven shillings a week. The new threshing machines threatened to put men out of work and into the poor houses, so they were the main targets of the rioters.

The farmhands destroyed some 97 machines in all, a higher figure than that recorded in any other county. The first instance was at All Cannings, and soon farmers in the Devizes area were removing or destroying the machines in an effort to appease the followers of Captain Swing as the rioters were known.

Farmers endeavouring to take out insurance against rick burning found the companies unsympathetic, and soon all threshing machines in the Salisbury area had been destroyed. In Devizes, the magistrates recommended an increase in wages to ten shillings a week. At Alton, near Pewsey, a farmer trying to defend his machinery fired on his assailants, wounding them. In retaliation, his furniture was destroyed, but he was not hurt. Some farmers tried to bribe the workers, but to no avail.

At last the Yeomanry Cavalry was brought in and one of the labourers, John Hardy, was shot dead and many were wounded. The revolt collapsed and three hundred and thirty six Wiltshiremen and three women stood trial at Salisbury in a three-week case, the largest in the whole of the south of England. Some ninety of those charged were liable to the death penalty, but the judges were inclined to mercy.

Fifty were sentenced to death, but this was commuted to transportation to Australia, with two exceptions, though they gained a last minute reprieve. Eventually a hundred and fifty were transported, forty-six went to prison and one hundred and thirty were acquitted.

Very few of the men transported to Australia returned home to Wiltshire — perhaps they took part in the Australian gold rush and died rich men.

THE ROAD WITH NO BEGINNING — OR END

It is typical of Wiltshire, with its ancient history, that one of its roads should have no beginning and no end, for such is the antiquity of the Ridgeway that traverses its boundaries.

The prehistoric trackway was a route used by the Stone Age people and its origins go back for more than six thousand years, and is believed to be one of the oldest trade paths in existence.

As the Ridgeway follows the undulations of the Downs in Wiltshire and on into Berkshire, it makes marvellous walking country for anyone seeking a continuous route for fifty or more miles.

The Ridgeway starts in course about four miles west of Marlborough and is a wonderful track that has endured for centuries. Walking along its rugged loneliness often with no habitation in sight for miles, it gives one a strange feeling of timelessness to realise that your feet are treading the same turf walked on by hundreds of generations. You are seeing the same hills, the same sky and traversing the same path and the sight of cows on a skyline resembles a frieze. It is as if one moves out of time and its very agelessness is its attraction.

For the imaginative, it can be eerie and lonely as dusk falls, and on pausing to listen, it is almost as if one hears again the tramp of Roman legions, or the jingle of harness as our forebears wended their way along the selfsame path.

ROBBERS' STONES

A forbidding looking stone stands on the highway just where the road from the Plain descends into West Lavington. The inscription gives a dire warning:

"At this spot Mr Dean of Imber was attacked and robbed by four highwaymen in the evening of October, 21, 1839. *After a spirited pursuit of three hours one of the Felons, Benjamin Colclough, fell dead on Chitterne Down. Thos Saunders, George Waters and Richard Harris were eventually captured, and were convicted at the ensuing Quarter Sessions at Devizes, and transported for a term of fifteen years. This monument is erected by public subscription as a warning to those who presumptuously think to escape the punishment God has threatened against Thieves and Robbers."*

A second, similar stone is erected about a mile across the downs from the Tilshead to Chitterne road. This reads:

"This Monument is erected to record the awful death of Benjamin Colclough, a Highway robber, who fell dead on this spot in attempting to escape his pursuers after robbing Mr Dean, of Imber, in the evening of October, 21, 1839, *and was buried at Chitterne, without funeral rites. The robbery of the wicked shall destroy them. Prov.* 21:7. *His three companions in Iniquity, Thomas Saunders, George Waters and Richard Harris were captured and sentenced at the ensuing Quarter Sessions at Devizes to Transportation in the Term of Fifteen Years. Though hand join in hand the wicked shall not be unpunished. Prov.* 11, 21.

ROUNDHOUSES

England in the nineteenth century, suffered much from lawlessness, so tiny, stone built Roundhouses or Blind Houses were built in many villages to serve as lock-ups. The local constable could restrain someone in such a place overnight or until they could be brought to justice.

Wiltshire has many such small lock-ups and the confined person was in the dark.

One is to be found at Shrewton, where it was carefully moved, stone by stone recently, and put in a place of safety in the village, away from the speeding traffic. Many a prisoner spent his last night on earth in this one, for there was a gibbet on which they were hung about a mile away.

Another well-known lock-up is at Bradford on Avon and another at Steeple Ashton and the village of Lacock possesses its blind house.

BATTLE OF ROUNDWAY DOWN, JULY 1643

Three hundred and thirty-three years ago, in the English autumn, a battle was fought in the depths of Wiltshire.

Sir William Waller, the Parliamentarian leader, only checked by the Battle of Lansdown in Bath, succeeded in cooping up the Royalists, under Prince Maurice, in Devizes.

For three days, there was a great siege with the Roundheads pouring cannon fire on to the town held by the Royalist forces. Prince Maurice held out, and Hopton, the gallant commander, though wounded, did not surrender (though he was offered terms) and the Royalist reinforcements arrived.

The Roundheads withdrew up the slopes of Roundway Down, thought by some Cavaliers to be a ruse to draw them out. However, it was decided to attack, and the enemy was heavily defeated by the loyal troops of King Charles I. The Roundhead cavalry was swiftly cut down and soon the whole army destroyed, leaving Prince Maurice free to join his Uncle, the King, at Oxford.

This lonely Hill, described as a "steepe place where never a horse went downe nor up before" proved to be a disastrous one for the Roundheads, for the Royalist cavalry broke their ranks and all that remained of the 1,800 Parliamentary infantry then surrendered, their officers riding rapidly away. With the destruction of Waller's army, the Battle of Roundway Down was considered the greatest cavalry victory of the Civil War.

Naturally, there was great rejoicing in the Royalist camp and the Cavaliers afterwards called the place, "Runaway Down" to commemorate the place where the enemy had indeed run away.

Their songsters wrote many rhymes and songs in celebration, one of which goes:

Go burn some rebel town for such alone
Are bonfires suited to the joys we own;
And let the falling ashes sprinkled lie
On traitors' heads; Let them repent and die.

The place where Waller crossed to take up his position on Roundway Hill, after leaving Chippenham, is known today as "Rowdeford" a reminder of where he forded the stream at Rowde.

Another reminder is an entry in the Rowde Parish Register which reads: "1643, July 13, being Thursday, was the great fight on Roundway Hill in which William

Bartlett was shot in the forehead and was buried in martial wise at Rowde. He was chief-quartermaster to the noble Colonel Sands and was baptised *ut patet*, 26 March 1615."

Even to this day, though the hill lies quiet and tranquil, many people believe the old legend and can hear the desperate hoofbeats as the defeated Roundheads charged down the hill in a frantic attempt to save their lives. The beaten men, clattering and stumbling — many to meet their deaths when their horses, unable to keep up the pace forced on them — stumbled and fell, to be buried in the Bloody Ditch at the foot of the hill or in neighbouring churchyards. Their cries are said to echo on a still night.

ROYAL ARTILLERY (SALISBURY PLAIN) HUNT

The Royal Artillery (Salisbury Plain) Hunt is said to be the only recognised pack of foxhounds maintained by a Regiment in England.

It was established in 1940 as a successor to the Royal Artillery Harriers which were formed in 1908 to hunt the southern part of the Tedworth country.

The kennels are at Larkhill and all hunt staff are amateurs.

A ROYAL GHOST

Mary Nicholas, of Manningford Bruce, helped her sister, Jane Lane, to save Charles II's life after the Battle of Worcester in 1651. Jane rode pillion behind the king, dressed as a groom, along roads thick with Parliamentarian troops determined to catch him. The brave woman led her sovereign safely through the enemy lines, helped by her sister.

In gratitude, Charles II granted the Nicholas family of Manningford Bruce, the rare privilege of bearing on their arms the three lions of England, as well as a scarlet horse. (This splendid coat of arms is to be found on a modest tablet in the Church of St Peter. It is one of the few churches to have an apse but no east window, and Mary Nicholas and her husband, Sir Edward, are buried in the chancel.)

Charles II is said to have stayed a night at Manningford Bruce Rectory during his escape, and in 1934, a guest sleeping in the room reputed to have been occupied by the King, awoke to see a group of men near the fireplace, one of whom resembled Charles II, all playing a game of chance. The terrified lady fell asleep and woke later to see the men still playing cards. The King was also "seen" in 1970, according to local sources.

A ROYAL VISIT TO THE CATHEDRAL

For the first time in its nine-hundred years, Salisbury Cathedral was honoured by the presence of the Sovereign, when Queen Elizabeth, accompanied by HRH the Duke of Edinburgh came to the City in April 1974 to present the annual Maundy Money.

In bright, spring sunshine, the Queen handed the traditional, specially minted money to forty-eight selected people from the County. Among them was a 95 year old Rowde woman, Mrs Beatrice Watts, the oldest person ever to receive the Maundy money.

ROYAL WILTSHIRE YEOMANRY

The Yeomanry Cavalry of Wiltshire, formed in 1791, as a precaution against the possibility of French invasion, was the oldest of the yeomanry regiments in England.

In 1831, it was awarded the title "Royal" and became the Royal Wiltshire Regiment of Yeomanry Cavalry, and awarded the new title of Prince of Wales's Own Royal Regiment in 1865 when it had the honour of providing an escort to the Prince of Wales.

Queen Victoria authorised a table of precedence for yeomanry cavalry regiments in 1884, and, as the first regiment formed, the Royal Wiltshire Yeomanry headed the list.

Unlike the Wiltshire Regiment, its infantry counterpart as it were, it has no VCs to its credit, though the Regimental Roll reads like a school register — The Thynnes, the Herberts, the Longs, the Fullers, the Awdrys and Palmers among them all saw service. The continuity of names bears witness to the devotion to duty and public spiritedness of the families who held lands in Wiltshire. There always seems to be a particular sense of friendship amongst its members in the Yeomanry, for, not only did its officers serve together on the battlefields of South Africa, France, El Alamein and Italy, they also hunted together in the Wiltshire fields in peacetime.

The blast of trumpets and the dust of war has died away leaving a fine record of service and achievement it would be hard to equal. The Regiment acquitted itself with honour and distinction in peace and war, and stand as a fine reminder of the Yeomen who have always served their country in days of trouble.

SALISBURY

Fair Salisbury, the capital of the county, is one of England's most attractive and interesting cities with a rich and fascinating history woven into the tapestry of its development.

Built on the confluence of four rivers and developed from Old Sarum, the Iron Age camp on a hill which later became a Roman Fortress and site of a Norman castle and cathedral, gradually it became Salisbury.

Essentially a market town, its first charter was granted in 1220, and its harmonious collection of buildings date from the fifteenth century to Georgian blendingly unifying into a wonderful entity.

Archbishop Poore planned the city in the thirteenth century on a medieval, chequered plan which remains with the Market Square as the centre and the Cathedral as the focal point. (*See also The Great Cathedral*).

Salisbury has so rich a heritage of historic buildings and associations, it is the more difficult to particularise, but for me, the Close and Cathedral in the centre, with those mellowed houses like gentle guardians of its beauty, is the part to which I could return again and again.

A variety of houses which do not crowd the scene, yet each in its own right seem to possess a claim to note which make up the whole, so exclusive that to reach it, one has to enter by a tall, oaken gate that has stood for centuries and is still closed at night.

The former Bishop's Palace, now a School dates from the thirteenth century, and of the many other fine buildings one is the Old Deanery which was built between 1258 and 1277 by Robert de Wykehampton when Dean of Salisbury. Today it is part of a fine group of buildings in the grounds of the College of Sarum St Michael, including a thirteenth century solar range, fifteenth century tower, thirteenth century Great Hall which still retains the original roof and central hearth, butteries and fifteenth century kitchen wings.

Mompesson House, one of the finest in the Close was built in 1701 for the Mompessons who were the merchants of the day and contains the original panelling and plasterwork.

In a corner of the Close is Malmesbury House, another Queen Anne building which still retains part of the original fourteenth century creation. For two hundred years the home of the Earls of Malmesbury, it has long musical associations, and it is said that Handel gave his first concert in England in the house in 1710.

In 1261 Bishop Giles de Bridport established the College of St Nicholas de Vaux, England's first university, but overshadowed later by Oxford, it fell into decay.

The great market square has been the scene of tragedy and triumph, for here a Duke of Buckingham was executed and celebrations for coronations and jubilees provided entertainment for all. The regular markets, first held in 1222, though the charter is dated 1227 continue to this day.

One of the unhappier places is no longer there, but its memory lingers. Fisherton Gaol was built in 1421 and included in 1631 a women's prison, said to be one of the County's Houses of Correction. In 1712, though it was claimed to be "one of the most commodious in England," this was not high praise. In 1800, it was converted into a county gaol, rebuilt in 1822 but finally pulled down in 1875. In its heyday, it was used as a place of execution, the last taking place in 1777.

Inevitably, the whole county is drawn to Salisbury and not only because of its great Cathedral. It remains the focal point, as it did when it was first built centuries ago, and one senses it will always be so.

FIRST SALVATION ARMY BAND

In the year 1878, the citizens of Salisbury went on strike. They had had enough — more than enough. It was too much for any to bear. For months the quiet atmosphere of the Cathedral city had been disturbed by the sound of "ooligans under the cloak of religion" who dared to sing and march and preach in the market place. They also dared to congregate at a joiner's shop they used as a mission hall to conduct services for passers-by.

To some, they sounded not so far removed from "the sound of a travelling menagerie."

Who were these people who so disturbed the tranquillity of the city? They called themselves Christian Missioners, and were led by a man and woman who went under the title of "Evangelists" and made their first appearance in March 1878.

Later, the *Salisbury and Winchester Journal* published a complaint written by those who signed themselves "Disgusted" and called the attention of readers to the disgraceful scene.

The Christian Mission was undeterred and became the Salvation Army in the autumn of that year, the Captain being Arthur Waite.

One Sunday evening, a crowd in the market square were surprised to see a group of four men with the Salvationists, each playing a brass instrument. There were two cornets, a valve trombone and an euphonium. It was from that quartet of musicians there grew the world-wide fraternity which now numbers tens of thousands. Four brave men facing a hostile crowd because they believed they were right.

The instrumentalists were Charles Fry and his three sons — Fred, Ernest and Bert, and their appearance was not part of a preconceived plan by General Booth.

The first Salvation Army Band came into being at Salisbury because the Fry family responded to the need for a bodyguard to defend the pioneers from rough handling by the citizens. The fact that they were militant Christians was of great importance, and the pattern and future of Army banding was established.

Charles William Fry was born on May 29th 1837. His mother was a Miss Hardiman whose father kept the "Green Dragon" at Aldbury, near Salisbury. Charles Fry, always musical, learned to play more than one instrument and was leader of an orchestra which played in the local chapel. When he was married, he played first cornet in the band of the 1st Wiltshire Volunteer Rifle Corps. His three sons were taught to play brass instruments almost as soon as they could hold them. The eldest, Fred, was installed as second cornet in the chapel orchestra, and when this was abandoned, was appointed organist, but prejudice had to be overcome. The citizens objected to the use of a drum on the streets of Salisbury on a Sunday, so it was played on weekdays only. One day, the drummer plucked up enough courage to play on Sundays and it was accepted and introduced into the Army. Sometimes, people could only afford a drum not a whole band, but it never lost its appeal.

The Fry family joined the Salvation Army at the suggestion of its Captain to help quell the disturbances at meetings by soothing them with music. The honour of being the first bandmaster in the Salvation Army belongs to Charles Fry and his eldest son is recognised as being the first bandsman.

After years of travelling and working for the Army, Charles Fry died in Glasgow in 1882 and a Monument to "The First Bandmaster of the Salvation Army" was unveiled on New Year's Day 1884.

Salisbury bandsmen again made history in December 1922 when the Band Vocal Quartet were the first Salvationist musicians to broadcast. A wireless pioneer possessed a special licence and broadcast a short programme from his home in the outskirts of the city, received at the city hall.

MARY SANDALL

The old line,

Where every tree might hold beneath
A Masked and pistolled rider.

was very true in the eighteenth century and Wiltshire had its share of highwaymen.

Though the law exacted a terrible penalty — hanging, for all offenders caught and convicted of highway robbing, this did not deter a young Wiltshire woman from leaving her native village at Baverstock and trying to imitate the exploits of a "gentleman of the road."

In her adventure, she was aided and abetted by the local blacksmith and weaver, who probably hoped to share the spoils, and bravely Mary Abraham, alias Mary Sandall, dressed herself in male clothing. Astride a fine horse, with pistols primed, she rode along the high roads near Wilton in search of adventure on a spring afternoon in 1779.

Mrs. Thring was walking along the turnpike road to North Burcombe, not far from her home, when along came Mary Sandall, brandished her pistol, and demanded money. Greatly surprised, but supposing there was no other course open to her, Mrs Thring surrendered all her movable property, consisting of "two shillings and a black silk cloak."

The highwayman insisted on her removing her rings and shoe buckles, but Mrs Thring declared her husband was in sight, so the robber clapped spurs to the horse and made off with all speed.

Mrs Thring immediately raised a hue and cry and it was not long before the thief was overtaken and captured. A pistol case and ammunition were found, but no pistol, which had been thrown over a hedge by Mary in her headlong flight. This was soon discovered and the girl brought before the magistrate.

The initial astonishment that the "highwayman" was a woman, gave way to greater surprise when everyone recognised her as Mary Abraham (alias Mary Sandall), well-known and well-liked in the district.

Mrs Thring swore to her identity and she was committed to Fisherton gaol to await her trial at Salisbury Assizes.

If the whole escapade had been planned as an adventure, it was not taken lightly by the authorities, and the weaver and blacksmith were questioned, and freely admitted lending her clothes and pistols, so were bound over to give evidence.

At the July Assizes, Mary was brought before Mr Baron Perrhyn and Mr Sergeant Heath and the case fully proved. Sentence of death was passed, but later respited, and the incident falls into obscurity.

Whether Mary Sandall was the victim of a clever plot or was a wilful girl seeking adventure will never be known, but it is certain she was a complete novice as a highwaywoman, and lucky to escape the dire consequences of her folly.

THE SPRING WHICH NEVER RUNS DRY

Urchfont, once described as a "picture-book" village has a long history, for it is recorded in the Domesday book, and its name originated from the word *funta* meaning a spring which never runs dry.

Certainly, it has all the classical needs for its description — a fine manor house built in the reign of William and Mary, once owned by William Pitt; and Georgian houses and thatched cottages in an attractive blend round a large duckpond, in which ducks still swim, and a village green.

The whole aspect of the village is pleasing for it has kept its charm over the centuries, retaining the best of the past, and losing nothing to modern times. A mellow example of a brick barn traditionally raised on staddle stones is one of the county's ingenuities, for it raised the barn so as to allow air to pass underneath, and perhaps more important, prevented rats from eating the grain inside.

The old coach road from Salisbury crosses the eastern boundaries after descending from the heights of Redhorn Hill. This is another wild, lonely stretch of the great Salisbury Plain, much used by the army these days, though when free of soldiery makes wonderful walking country. It seems to stretch to infinity and it is possible to traverse its ruggedness to Salisbury's outskirts.

JANE SEYMOUR

Wulfhall in the heart of Savernake Forest, the Uefale of *Domesday* came to the Seymours by marriage in the reign of Henry VI. Sir John Seymour, Chief Ranger of the Forest, and father of Jane Seymour, lived there.

Born at Wulfhall in 1509, Jane Seymour was a perfect daughter — small, meek, dutiful and obedient, and these qualities supported her throughout her life towards her great ambition. This was to ensnare the great Tudor King, Henry VIII. That this brown-eyed little maid from Wiltshire could capture the love of the King of England was an achievement, the more so as it meant the downfall of the beautiful and vivacious Anne Boleyn, already his wife.

Jane first came to Court as lady-in-waiting to Queen Catherine of Aragon, and became Anne Boleyn's attendant after Catherine's divorce. Submissive and affable, she must have seemed angelic compared to the wilful Queen and a haven of peace to King Henry. She flirted and encouraged the King, so that, when Anne had been executed she was ready to wed her Sovereign without, it seems, thought or pity for her predecessor.

Before their wedding Henry came often to Savernake Forest and courted Jane amid the great oaks that flourished. In fact, their "wedding feast" is said to have been celebrated in a barn at Wulfhall especially hung with tapestry for the occasion — but unhappily, the house and barn are no more.

Henry VIII married his third wife, Jane, in Whitehall and some nine months later she was pregnant. Her position was secure and she determined to bear the king a living son. Jane was cosseted and cared for with all the skill the physicians could muster and, to everyone's great joy, gave birth to the son and heir, Prince Edward, on October 12th 1537. There was tremendous rejoicing and the King was beside himself with joy.

The feastings soon turned to sorrow, for the labour had been difficult and soon it was realised that Jane's life was in danger. Feverish and dying, Jane was carried to her son's christening, on a litter draped with ermine, some twelve days after his birth. On October 24th, Jane died and Henry was inconsolable, ordering that on his death his body should be placed beside that of Jane.

The girl from Wiltshire had achieved her ambition — to marry Henry VIII and bear him a living son who was later to become King of England. Her son, for whom she had suffered so much, died at the early age of sixteen, and his mother's family remained in Wiltshire, her father being buried in Great Bedwyn Church.

SHEPHERDS AND SHEEP

The rich, rolling downland has been ideal for sheep farming, and for years, the shepherds and their flocks roamed freely across the wide stretches. Though much of the land is now fenced in, sheep are still to be seen in many areas, though the custom of fixing sheep bells to their necks has died out.

Shepherds were important people, respected by all as the undoubted king of all farmworkers, and his sheep took precedence over other animals. A shepherd never allowed his lambs to be counted before lambing time was over, it was considered unlucky to do so.

In the past, sheep bells belonged to the shepherd, not the farmer, and were often buried with him, and he was frequently buried with a piece of lamb's wool entwined in his fingers, to explain to his Maker why, as a shepherd, he had missed church services because of his flock.

Wiltshire's special sheep were a long-legged breed, known as the Wiltshire Horn and was very popular at one time.

George III took a special interest in Wiltshire sheep. He was very impressed when he saw a flock in the county and appointed the shepherd, Richard Daphney, to be shepherd of his royal flock at Windsor.

Some time later two sheep were missing and the king was most upset, though he would not press charges. Daphney said, "If I cannot serve my king with a crook, I will with a musket," and joined the Guards.

One of the county's most revered shepherds was David Saunders, known as the "humble shepherd of Salisbury Plain." He was born in Lavington in 1717 and died in 1796 and is buried in West Lavington churchyard. He was said to have been one of Wesley's converts and became totally blind before he died.

His story is told in Hannah Moore's *Shepherd of Salisbury Plain.*

SILBURY HILL

Strange, brooding and somehow majestic, Silbury Hill rises, somewhat surprisingly to a height of some 130 feet. It stands a little way back from the main road to Marlborough amid a host of grey wethers and with the West Kennett longbarrow almost opposite Avebury is but round the corner.

The whole place is steeped is antiquity and some say it is another of Wiltshire's early religious centres. It is the largest man-made mound in Europe, and covers an area of some five acres, with a diameter of just over an hundred feet across its flat top. It was said to have been built about 2,600 BC.

It was estimated that between eight and nine million cubic feet of chalk were moved to make it, and the hill constructed in six circular steps, each smaller than the one beneath.

It is, like Stonehenge, another of Wiltshire's mysteries. No one knows why it was built, though a popular theory is that it was a burial mound. Legend says that King Sil was buried there on horseback, and others believe there is a lifesize figure of solid gold, or even a king on a golden coffin, but excavations have revealed nothing.

Long, long ago it was felt the hill was an evil place and a construction of the Devil where black magic had been practised. In 1849, a stone circle was found giving substance to this claim, and thinking the best way to be rid of this evil was by burying it, this was done. Excavations carried out in 1968, revealed some isolated boulders but nothing else of significance.

Kings and Queens have stopped to climb this strange hill and look with pleasure over a wide expanse of Marlborough downland. Among them, in 1683, King Charles II and his brother, James, climbed to the top, but Queen Catherine watched from her carriage.

Long, long ago there was a quarrel between the men of Marlborough and the men of Devizes. Realising that numerically they were much weaker than their enemy, the men of Marlborough enlisted the aid of the Devil.

He was quite willing to help, and picking up a large hill, carried it in his apron to drop it on Devizes. The people of the town were very frightened when they heard he was on his way, and as St John happened to be in the neighbourhood, appealed to him for help.

The saint told them to collect together all their old boots and put them in a sack. When this was done, he handed the sack to the oldest inhabitant and gave him some instructions, sending him to meet the Devil. He set off and the two met.

"Pardon me." said the old man. "Will you tell me the time of the day?"

The Devil was cross. Not only was he carrying a very heavy load, but he had a blister on his foot, and his tail was uncomfortable because he had tucked it into his pocket.

"I don't know the time," he said petulantly, "how far is it to Devizes?" "Oh, it's a very long way to Devizes," replied the old man. "I left there years ago and have been walking ever since." He opened the sack to display the contents and said, "See all these old boots, I've worn them out on my journey."

This threw the Devil into a rage. He had no idea that Devizes was such a long way off. In his temper he threw down his load and disappeared in a burst of flame.

The hill he dropped is there to this day and known as Silbury Hill.

One old custom, which has died out, was that on Palm Sunday, all the villagers from round and about, visited the hill, singing and dancing and feasting on figs and cider.

Nestling near the foot of the hill is an old, old coaching inn — the Waggon and Horses, visited by Dickens and featured by him in the "Bagman's Tale." It was particularly popular in the old days when coach travellers stopped there for refreshment before setting out on the often hazardous journey across the bleak downs to reach Marlborough. In bad weather, many preferred to seek shelter for the night beneath its walls, as more than one coach stuck in snowdrifts and the occupants perished. To this day, it is still a welcome place for the traveller.

A SIMPLE COUNTRY CHURCH

If you walk into the little, white church of St Mary at Dilton, or more familiarly, Old Dilton, you will be forgiven for thinking you have gone back into time.

Of fourteenth century origin, with a stone spirelet, this little church has remained untouched since Georgian times, and is a perfect example of how a simple, country church looked two hundred years ago.

The eighteenth century furnishings, the plain bleached box pews, three decker pulpit, large family pews, and two small galleries, one looking directly into the chancel are unchanged. Somehow, today's congregation are the ones who seem in fancy dress, not the setting for their worship.

SIMNEL CAKE

This was particularly popular in Wiltshire in the eighteenth and nineteenth centuries when servant girls traditionally took one home to their mothers on Mothering Sunday, and is still made and enjoyed to this day, very often at Easter.

The name originated from two children — Simon and Nellie — who had differing tastes in cooking. Simon liked his cake boiled and Nellie hers baked so their enterprising mother devised one that was a combination of both methods.

Basically, the cake is a fruit one, with a layer of marzipan on top and in the centre, but is never iced. Nowadays, it is topped with saffron and decorated with eggs, chickens or flowers and tied with a wide ribbon. It may take a little time to make (and these days there is no boiling!) but it tastes delicious.

THE SMALLEST POWER STATION

Downton is a large and beautiful place with one very long, very wide street, and a band of grass that separates the cottages from the road.

Opposite an old cross is an inn with two ancient wooden busts of King John and Queen Isabella, set in niches, and said to commemorate the King's visits.

Three bridges have to be crossed to see the Tannery, complete with a water wheel and opposite is what is claimed to be the smallest power station in England.

FARMER SNOOK OF BLUNSDON

In former days, the village of Blunsdon had a rather special hero. He was a Farmer Snook who obtained great fame by his claim that he had had twenty-one children *twice*.

The truth was that after the birth of his twenty-first child, followed by its early death, yet another baby was produced by his long-suffering wife, so for the second time, he could proudly state that he was the father of twenty-one children!

This achievement does not seem to have resulted in financial reward for poor Farmer Snook was very poor and died owing a great deal of money. In fact, the story goes that his creditors, anxious to lose no chance of recouping their money, even stopped his corpse on the way to burial and held it at ransom, until for shame, one of the mourners repaid a little of the debt.

SIX WELLS

Legend has it that King Alfred, his soldiers round him, was exhausted from his long battles with the invading Danes, and knelt down and prayed for refreshing water. In a valley to the West of the village of Stourton, six wells, or springs, appeared. Refreshed, the King and his army went on to great victories.

SNOB'S HORSE

Wiltshire is famed for its White Horses laboriously cut into the downs, the chalk making a perfect material for such artistry.

At Whitsuntide in 1848, the shoemakers of Devizes cut a horse on the slopes of Roundway Hill. For many years this was known as the "Snob's Horse" the word *snob* being used in more than one provincial dialect for a shoemaker's journeyman, and appearing also in the form of *snob* in Lowland Scottish for an apprentice to that trade.

No signs of this figure are now visible, nor are there any traces of another small horse cut into the slopes near Pewsey.

STONEHENGE

Stonehenge, older than Time itself, has stood magnificent upon the wild, brooding Wiltshire Downs for more than a thousand years before the pyramids. Approached from any direction, it must be an awe-inspiring sight, even to those, like myself, who have seen it often and never failed to be impressed by its majesty.

Silent and apart, strange and brooding, it has defied the ravages of men and time and still kept its secrets. In all centuries, there have been those who have looked and wondered, yet none can claim the real answer. Why was it built? How did it get there?

Those stones, some upright, some horizontal, have remained in their majestic circle, it seems, since the world began, and yet human hand must have toiled in their creation.

Even from a distance, they are clearly visible against their marvellous downland background which shows them to full advantage. And they never seem in any way diminished, yet in close up, they are fearsome in their glory.

The encircling ditch bank and holes are Neolithic, and there are stone circles of sarsen stones around a horseshoe of Trilithons encompassing blue stones with early Bronze Age altar stones.

Stonehenge is unique. Nowhere in the world is there anything resembling its grandeur and Wiltshire-men are rightly proud of this, their finest inheritance. It must be said they are quietly proud, they are glad it is theirs, and theirs alone, and something that no one can equal or take away. Beside it, men seem small in stature and many of the great men of the world have come to wonder. It is said it is impossible to count the massive stones, and legend claims that, after his flight from the Battle of Worcester when Charles II stayed a night at Zeals, he paused to wile away his time awaiting ship for France by counting (or trying to) the great stones.

The great Sarsen Circle about one hundred feet in diameter, originally consisted of some thirty upright stones, each weighing about twenty-five tons, capped by a continuous ring of thirty lintels weighing about seven tons. Inside was a pair of Sarsen Trilithons, each trilithon consisting of a pair of huge uprights, weighing up to forty-five tons, capped by a massive lintel.

Many believe, as I do, that Stongehenge has deeply religious connections and I am always conscious of a feeling of "presence" whenever I visit it. For me, it especially brings home the insignificance of man compared to the majesty of God, and the Druid ceremonies on Midsummer Day seem pagan in comparison, and it is up to the individual to make his own decisions, The Druids were, of course, a Celtic priesthood, and it is said there is no evidence to support the claims that some of the stones were used for human sacrifices.

Much legend attaches to so great a place, Geoffrey of Monmouth suggested that the stones were really giants, turned into stone for some misdemeanour, and like Lot's wife, condemned to stand frozen for ever on a bleak and windy Plain in Wiltshire.

Naturally, the superstitious claim that the fall of stone is a dreadful portent of doom, and it was said that, if a lintel fell, it meant the death of a monarch and a writer in an American newspaper (where else?) tried to show that the fall of a stone foretold the deaths of Edward I and II, James II, Queen Anne, George II and IV and William IV. The fall of one upright and one lintel of the outer sarsen circle on the last night of the nineteenth century (*The Times*, 3rd January, 1901) was interpreted to represent the death of Queen Victoria which occurred on the 22nd January of that year.

The Stonehenge Bird is another well-known story. At daybreak on Midsummer Day 1894 a bird is reputed to have perched on the Heel stone and flown away a moment before the sun rose over the stone. Legend says that this is often the case, and for the rest of the year no bird is ever known to alight on this stone.

These great stones will always attract interest In the past, many believed they held healing properties and to touch them would bring relief to sufferers. Even today, some touch them "for luck", and of course, the legendary Merlin, so known in these parts, is always associated with Stonehenge.

Everyone who sees the monument will draw their own conclusions. Some come to look and wonder, others to gaze in awe at its magnificence and beauty, and who can fail to be moved by its majesty, its seeming aloofness. To me, it stands supreme, and as a Moonraker, gives one a sense of continuity to know that however far one wanders, even abroad, Stonehenge will be there to welcome one home. It is this quality of timelessness that gives the county its strength and puts life into perspective, for, long after this generation is but a memory, Stonehenge will endure and, probably in a thousand years hence, still give men cause to wonder and respect.

STOURHEAD

Another of Wiltshire's many beauties lies in the south, about three miles from Mere.

Standing in magnificent gardens which are said to be quite unique and outstanding in both England and Europe as an example of the eighteenth century landscape gardens, is Stourhead House, home of the Hoare family since 1772.

The grounds, so carefully planned and laid out in the eighteenth century, are so designed that they form an entity which can be seen by a walk round the lake. Originally, the river Stour, which rises nearby, formed a series of ponds and, by building a dam, these were converted into a lake, the banks of which house a Grotto, and the great Pantheon completed in 1754.

A stone bridge, copied from Palladio, was erected in 1762, and the Bristol Cross dated 1575 taken from the City of Bristol makes a picturesque point of arrival or departure and is clearly seen from the other side of the lake.

Other delights in the gardens which, in high summer, abound in flowers, are the Rustic Cottage, Temple of Apollo and another Bristol monument known as St Peter's Pump. Always, they seem fresh and enriching and the work of those patient planners who had the courage and foresight to create them two centuries ago is well rewarded.

Probably because of the beauty of the gardens, the house seems overshadowed, but, once inside there is much of interest with beautifully proportioned rooms, furniture and pictures to captivate. It certainly has a most imposing background.

LORD STOURTON — MURDERER

The eighth Lord Stourton, Lord Lieutenant of the County of Wiltshire murdered two of his servants in 1557. For this crime he was hanged in Salisbury Market Place. His rank gave him the privilege of being hanged with a silken rope.

STRUCK BY LIGHTNING

A heraldic wall monument in the 14th century church in the scattered village of Nettleton has a rare distinction. It was struck by lightning, bearing the marks to this day, and is the only known church in the county to have been so afflicted.

The monument was to Samuel Arnold, a nineteenth century Rector for forty years, and was struck in 1842, the damage being repaired by the parishioners. Arnold and another nineteenth century Rector, Charles Domville, shared, between them, the whole of the nineteenth century, the latter being there for fifty-eight years.

Apart from its damage, the church possesses one of the most beautiful church towers in the county. It is one of a group in which one of the bells has been ringing for five hundred years.

Yet another record attaches to this village — the Nettleton Tumulus in a field on the Roman Fosse Way here, a long, green mound with three rugged stones on top is one of the oldest monuments in England. Recessed into a cliff is the site of a Roman temple to the goddess Diana which is still preserved. Maybe it was this pagan temple which brought Divine wrath in the shape of lightning to the village!

THE TWENTIETH LORD SUFFOLK

Charlton Park was the home of a very brave man. The twentieth Lord Suffolk was killed in 1941, dying a hero, but he was also a brilliant scientist and a trusted member of the British Intelligence Service.

Lord Suffolk was only thirty-five when he was killed, but in his short life he had shown amazing talent. He had been to Dartmouth, served as a Guards

Officer and sailed round the world before the mast as a mercantile marine apprentice. He went to Australia, working as a rancher, and at thirty-two took his degree at Edinburgh University with first-class honours in pharmacology.

When the Second World War broke out, Lord Suffolk was debarred from active service by the effects of an attack of rheumatic fever and he overcame any disability by sheer grit and determination. Unable to serve in the army, he did war work of a far more dangerous nature. His knowledge of the world of scientific research enabled him to learn that the Allies were using a particular, very secret chemical, the only supply of which was in Norway.

The Germans attacked this country to gain the chemical, but when they took the area, the stuff had already been removed to Paris. France fell, but undeterred, Lord Suffolk, on his own initiative, and with great daring, seized the whole supply and brought it to Bordeaux. He boarded a French ship, demanded an escort and a machine gun and sailed for England.

He then took up his work detonating unexploded bombs, working with a very small and efficient team. He met all hazards with amazing coolness and clarity of purpose, often dictating to his secretary while defusing a bomb. He would calmly smoke a cigarette until almost on top of the bomb on which he had to work, often handing it to someone to hold until he had finished.

For about six months, Lord Suffolk was engaged on this work, then he and his team were killed together. He received a posthumous award of the George Cross "for conspicuous bravery."

His name will long be remembered for, as is said of the brave, "by their deeds ye shall know them."

THE SQUIRREL AT CHERHILL

In 1882, a Mr David Eatwell stood at the foot of the Lansdowne Monument at Cherhill, and "watched a squirrel run right to the very top". The monument stands 125 feet high!

SWARM OF GNATS

In Wiltshire, gnats often swarm in vast numbers numbers resembling smoke!

On several occasions the Salisbury Cathedral fire alarm has been sounded when columns of gnats swarmed round the tall spire looking like dense smoke. This is recorded as happening in 1736 and the last recorded date for this odd occurrence was the 12th June 1952.

WILLIAM HENRY FOX TALBOT

This famous early pioneer of photography, though he was not born in Wiltshire, served the county as Member of Parliament for Chippenham, before retiring from politics and living as a country squire at Lacock Abbey. There, he devoted himself to his photographic experiments.

Always interested in photogenic drawing as it was called, he began by making his famous "mousetrap" cameras in 1835.

In 1840 he invented the first calotype and produced positive pictures from negatives.

For years, he continued with his experiments, photographing, his home and family, and the beautiful village of Lacock where he lived. Many of the estate workers featured in his early "snaps" and so have been given to posterity.

The very first photograph was the inside of a lattice window in Lacock Abbey which he took in August 1835, and in 1844 his book of some twenty-four calotype illustrations taken at Lacock was produced, and was the first ever photographically illustrated book.

The sixteenth century barn at the gates of Lacock Abbey has been converted into the Fox Talbot Photographic Museum, and on view are displays of photographs and letters, his dark room and early equipment, to make a lasting memorial to this great man.

THATCH HOOKS AT WEST LAVINGTON

If you drive too quickly through the village of West Lavington, you might miss an unusual sight!

Fixed to the side of a wall in the village are two enormous hooks which might easily be mistaken — for the masts of a sailing boat. In fact, they are thatch hooks, often used in the days when cottages were all thatched, and the only way of dealing with a fire was to pull the thatch quickly from the building. The size of the hooks makes one realise that firemen in those days must have possessed immense strength, but were probably used by a group of men for their length makes them very heavy and unwieldy.

ST THOMAS' PATH

One of England's martyrs, the great Thomas a Becket is closely associated with Wiltshire, for, in his early years as a priest, he lived in the parish of Winterbourne Earls. Part of his duties was to walk to Clarendon regularly to conduct mass.

The path he traversed was always green, even in wintertime, and is known as St Thomas' Path.

A THOUSAND YEARS OF WORSHIP

The sloping, open village of Dinton lies in the Nadder Valley, one of the loveliest parts of the county, and possesses an ancient British fort.

However, it is its church approached along a path arched by yew trees, that is one of the loveliest in Wiltshire. Nearly a thousand years old, the fabric dates from the twelfth century and some added in the fourteenth and fifteenth centuries. A brass in the vestry is dated 1710 and a square Norman font still stands on stumpy legs of Purbeck marble.

TOLLARD ROYAL

On the border with Dorset lies a beautiful village where King John is said to have spent much of his time between 1200 and 1213. He loved hunting in the woods and had a hunting lodge at Cranbourne Chase.

Steeped in beauty and legend, Tollard became Royal when King John granted it a royal charter, and his house, some of it thirteenth century, is a delight — the old wood and stone combining to give it a truly medieval air.

The ancient larner tree — a wych elm — was the site of the meetings of the Court Leet and, by tradition, the place where the King met his huntsman.

The village church contains an interesting effigy of Sir William Payne who died in 1588. He lies with drawn sword and his feet resting on a lion, clad in bonded mail which is very rare.

The stone walled well is of great age, but is still in working order.

The "small and ancient borough" of Marlborough as it used to be called, rose like a phoenix from the ashes of the great fire of 1653 which destroyed many of its buildings.

Nowadays, it is said to possess the most beautiful street in England and few could dispute this, for the great, wide, sloping street that is its main feature is superb.

Its history goes back to prehistoric times for the Castle Mound, said to be a smaller version of Silbury Hill, formed, from the eleventh century, part of the royal castle which flourished there. King John was said to favour this place and spend much of his time there, hunting in the great forest nearby, and was married in the Castle Chapel of St Nicholas.

Henry III summoned the Parliament to the Castle Precincts in 1267 when the Statute of Marlborough, which embodied certain of the demands of Simon de Montfort, was passed.

As time passed, the Castle flourished, but, during the Wars of the Roses, it declined and fell into disrepair, the site passing to the Seymour family who, in 1612 built a family mansion there.

The mansion, built by the Duke of Somerset, in 1770 became the Castle Inn some fifty years later and flourished during the heyday of the stagecoach. Many famous people stayed there on their way to take the waters of Bath, and the house remained a coaching inn until 1843 when it became the nucleus of Marlborough College.

There is much of interest to be found in this town where the College is a dominating feature, giving the place an air of tranquillity, resembling the peace and stature of a university town.

Marlborough was in turmoil in the Civil War, the town and castle taking opposite sides, the former supporting the Roundheads and Lord Seymour holding the castle for his King. Few towns suffered more from the War, possibly because of its proximity to Oxford from where the Cavaliers made constant attacks. A major assault was launched by the Royalists in December 1642 when much damage to buildings resulted, some of it still visible on the church towers. The King's Cause was triumphant and over a hundred prisoners taken to Oxford, but the Royalist stay was short, for a relieving force of Roundheads came from Newbury and re-took the town. The town saw more fighting as the war progressed and King Charles himself stayed there in 1644, when it was decided to fortify the town, though the plan was abandoned.

During the Commonwealth, disaster struck. In April 1653, as bark was drying in the house of a tanner, it caught fire so quickly the flames spread to other houses, and soon the south side of the town was ablaze. "The fire came with such force and vehemence the like was never seen in England before" said one report. Raging, the fire burned houses on both sides of the street sweeping them into one great inferno — inns, taverns, gentlemen's houses, shops, nothing was spared for some two hundred and fifty houses were destroyed, three hundred families made homeless and £70,000 worth of property in ruins. Cromwell ordered relief collections to be made throughout the Kingdom, and within a year the town was largely rebuilt, though, in view of the expense, the assizes were not included and the town lost some of its importance.

Further serious fires in 1679 and 1690 resulted in an Act of Parliament forbidding for ever the use of thatched roofs in Marlborough.

In spite of the devastation, much has survived, some of the buildings dating from Tudor times, and the High Street today is a pleasant blend of past and present, with the very old still retaining its domination.

Georgian buildings on both sides nestle with Tudor ones, and a bookshop of this period has a side passage leading to Back Lane which was formerly known as Horse Passage. In days past, it made a good escape route for thieves robbing merchants in the markets and fairs!

Though once described as "about the coldest place in the country," it possesses an air of serenity and distinction, and the quiet waters of the Kennet flowing softly in the meadows add to its peace.

A town that has overcome adversity, it presents the appearance of a place that will endure for ever. I hope so.

TRACKLEMENTS

A few years ago, a new name was added to those of Wiltshire delicacies, and something that began in a village, after which they were named, has blossomed into a national product.

An enterprising Calne lady decided to offer something new to serve with meats and so "Tracklements" appeared. These Urchfont mustards (after the village where they were made and sold) are subtly blended to enrich pies, hams and meats. Alternatively, a gourmet may prefer the herb jellies now made in the village of Easterton, ranging from mint, thyme and sage and made from apple juice which gives them their special flavour.

These additives soon caught the imagination of the public and, when in London, it is a pleasure to see a touch of "home" with the mustards and jellies on sale in shops that are "by Royal appointment."

A TREASURE AT PLACE FARM

Tisbury, set in wooded countryside in the sparkling Nadder Valley is steeped in romance.

The old church dates back to AD 674 and Rudyard Kipling is buried in the churchyard where there is a magnificent yew tree a thousand years young, and holding between the great, split trunk, a huge boulder.

The High Street follows the exact line of the early Saxon trackway from the Dorset Coast to the Severn estuary, and as it was built on solid rock, is almost unaltered.

However, it is Place Farm, formerly a grange of Shaftesbury Abbey, is part of one of the most interesting groups of fifteenth century buildings in England. One of its most prized possessions is the massive tithe barn which is nearly two hundred feet in length. It is claimed to be the second largest in England. over five hundred years old, and to renew the thatch would need nearly fifteen hundred square yards of thatch!

A TRIPLE GHOST STORY

Over four and a half centuries have passed since Littlecote House was built in Tudor times a little way from Ramsbury, and it has become one of the most famous haunted houses in this country.

Three of its ghosts have their origin in the same horrifying tale.

On a wet night in November 1575, a Mrs Barnes, the local midwife, was blindfolded and taken to a large house to attend to a woman in a mask, who was in labour. ,

No sooner was the child born than a man "of haughty and ferocious countenance" seized the baby from the midwife's arms, and in spite of the mother's piteous cries, pushed it into the red-hot embers of the fire with the heel of his boot.

The midwife, shocked and horrified, cut a small piece of cloth from the bedhanging, and it was this scrap of evidence that brought William Darrell of Littlecote to trial for murder Some say that by bribing the judge, Sir John Popham (whose family subsequently became owners of the house), Darrell evaded punishment.

However, Darrell's end was violent enough. His horse shied, some say frightened of the ghost of the Burning Baby, at a place known as Darrell's style, which is now frequented by his ghost and his phantom hounds. Horses still shy when passing this place.

The chamber in which the child was murdered is haunted by the spectre of a sad-looking woman carrying a baby in her arms.

These three ghosts are said to share the haunting of this house with others for a woman is frequently seen in the gardens and is believed to be Mrs Laybourne Popham, another visits the Chinese bedroom and a lady with a rushlight is visible. Others claim that a tenant, Gerard Bevin, who lived there after the Great War, and went to prison for embezzlement, haunts the Long Gallery.

ROBERT TROTMAN

In Kinso churchyard in Dorset is a headstone bearing the following inscription :

To the Memory of Robert Trotman, late of Rowde in the County of Wilts, who was barbarously murdered on the shore near Poole on the 24th March 1760.

A little tea, one leaf I did not steal
For Guiltless blood shed I to God appeal
Put Tea in one scale human blood in T'other
And think what tis to slay thy harmless brother.

Tradition says that he was a smuggler and met his death in an affray with the coastguards.

THE TRUFFLE HUNTERS

In the reign of Elizabeth I, a Spaniard was said to have settled in the village of Winterslow, bringing with him some rather special dogs. These animals were trained to smell out the underground, tuber-like fungus of the truffles which became a great delicacy.

The truffles are an edible, underground fungus which mature in the autumn and winter which is the time the experts were busy searching them out. A prized delicacy. they vary in size from hazel nuts to teacups, and the record is said to have been one weighing over two pounds.

Poodle dogs were said to be especially adept at sniffing out these delicacies, and Bill Collins was a very well-known expert in the ffeld, his family practising their craft for generations, until they gave up in the 1930s. Bill was said to wear a special uniform provided by the Earl of Radnor.

In 1860, the truffle hunters petitioned Parliament that "their dogs be exempted from the 12 shilling tax."

The small, terrier type of dog was often used being trained from puppyhood how to sniff out the truffles which his master would dig up, and the dog rewarded. Oak trees were good places, and often, in Victorian days, a man could make up to five shillings a day on truffles — a fortune when his wages were probably only ten shillings a week.

Truffles are still found overseas, and one of the problems in training dogs these days is the expense of smearing the puppy's face with expensive, imported truffles to make him used to the scent. One method of locating truffles is to watch a particular tree, where they are suspected, and if a swarm of small, yellow flies hover above a certain spot, it is worth digging to make sure.

In Victorian times, when they were plentiful and relatively cheap, truffles were often used in the stuffing of pheasants, fillings for omelettes or as an extra in meat pies.

TIMOTHY TUGMUTTON

In a firm hand, the name of TIMOTHY TUGMUTTON is written clearly on a blank leaf opposite the Easter Vestry minutes in the Seend Churchwardens' Books for the year 1712.

Someone suggested that it was written — perhaps to try a pen — by Ambrose Awdry, Junior, whose hand it somewhat resembles. He was one of the signers of the minutes, but none could prove his hand wrote the names opposite! If he did, maybe he still laughs at his little joke from another place, or maybe the real Timothy Tugmutton smiles that no one suspected him!

HANNAH TWYNNOY

In 1703, she was torn to pieces by a tiger in an exhibition of wild beasts at the White Lion Inn, at Malmesbury.

Her memorial reads:

"In bloom of youth she's snatched from hence
She had not room to make defence
For tyger fierce snatched life away
Until the Resurrection Day."

VILLAGE OF THE BELLS

Aldbourne, for me, personifies all that is attractive in a country village, for it has a duckpond, village green, an ancient cross and a village pump.

It is a very old, very interesting place wlth evidence of its continual occupation since the Bronze Age, and the population has remained constant, at two thousand people, for many years.

By Domesday, the village is recorded as possessing a well established fair with its own Court of Summary, and by 1311, a flourishing market on the green every week, where they also held religious feasts, and joustings and entertainments.

The focal point, as in most places, is of course, its wonderful fifteenth century church with a fifteenth century tower, an embattled parapet, and crocketed, pinnacled buttresses dating from 1460. There is a Norman doorway, some excellent monuments including one for two brothers whose joint lifespan was one hundred and eighty years, for Edward was ninety-six and his "young" brother, William, eighty-four when they died.

Thomas Goddard, resplendent in sixteenth century armour, is shown kneeling with a daughter and three bearded sons looking into the panelled arch of a medieval chapel, with his father's helmet above him.

The brasses include one to a priest, Henry Frekylton, who died in 1508, shown in his vestments. To complete the picture and given a "modern" touch, are two eighteenth century fire waggons, known locally as "Adam" and Eve".,

Aldbourne was once noted for its bell foundry which was famous throughout Wiltshire, supplying most of of the area with bells. The brothers Corr came to Aldbourne in 1684 working as wooden button makers, a trade they continued while casting some eight-eight large bells.

Other industries followed — straw plaiting, thatching, agriculture, hurdle making, rope and fustian among them. Most of the houses, many with a thatched roof have a history of their own.

Aldbourne Chase, a beautiful place, was said to have been a favourite hunting ground for King John and to which John of Gaunt was a frequent visitor. During the Civil War, it was the scene of a skirmish which the Sealed Knot re-enacted, in full colour, about four years ago.

The inns are old — the Blue Boar dates from 1460 with a legend that relates in 1516, No 8 bell was upturned and filled with beer outside the inn when it was dedicated.

The Crown was a staging post in the eighteenth century and the stables and ostlers' rooms remain with mounting block and a blowing stone. It is said the George Inn became an inn in the seventeenth century, and the Manor Court or Court Leet was held there in 1737.

There is much to see and cherish in this thriving Wiltshire village which, today, still offers its inhabitants the same opportunities for work and pleasure — in that they find their own — as in days long gone.

One always remembers pleasant things for the mind clouds over unhappiness, but, in a host of memories of Aldbourne, there is one July morning which will remain fresh for me. It was the Sunday on which the skirmish at Cranborne Chase was re-enacted and Morning Service at the lovely Church was unforgettable. The Church was filled and Members of the Sealed Knot, in Cavalier costume blended as naturally with the surroundings as did their solemnly dressed Roundhead opponents. The atmosphere was one of hope, the singing lifted the rafters and it was a truly uplifting experience, enhanced by the feeling that one had stepped back in time to the Civil War, when men worshipped in the selfsame way in this selfsame place.

THE VILLAGE OF THE STAPLE

The proud tower of the magnificent church of St Mary of Steeple Ashton is visible for miles, and was once described as "resembling a great ship sailing over the meadows."

The village in which it stands was once a wool market town, and originally known as Staple Ashton to mark the stone pillar which is in the centre as a symbol of the wool market established there by Royal Charter in 1349. The name was later changed to Steeple because of the church tower on the fine, five hundred year old church, one that owes its beauty to the wool trade, for clothiers provided the money for its building.

The steeple rose to one hundred and eighty-six feet, but was struck by lightning in 1670, and fell.

The church itself, a perfect example of the perpendicular style of fifteenth century architecture is regarded as a classic. It possesses an almost unique feature for English churches, the whole interior was designed to be vaulted in stone and the aisles were so completed, but the nave vault is of wood with elaborate vaulting. Fine palimpsest brasses adorn the walls, and the whole building gives one a true sense of peace.

The long street and old, timbered houses, some red brick and herringbone, cluster round a little green to make this village one of charm and character. A cross, established in 1671, but repaired in 1714, is set upon this green, set on stone thought to have been there at the time of the Conquest.

The traditional village lockup is octagonal and knobbed with a domed roof and no windows.

Many wool villages fell into decay with the decline of the wool trade, but not Steeple Ashton which preserves a true sense of continuity. One hopes it will always be there.

THE VILLAGE WITH TWO STEEPLES

Driving from Devizes to Marlborough can be an exhilarating experience. The long, straight road, with no hedges to distract, gives the urge to accelerate, but to do so would mean the loss of, to me, one of the finest views in the county. On one side, the great Wansdyke rises and swells into the broad sweep of the Marlborough Downs, and the Cherhill Monument stands proudly erect on the other. Some days, a line of racehorses in training is etched against the early morning skyline. If a town can be a melody in stone, then surely this view is a melody in majesty.

Forming part of this landscape and nestling among the trees and houses, rise the two spires of Bishops Cannings Church, making a perfect setting for a Constable painting.

In the very heart of the county, it was the setting for the Moonraker Legend, and is a typical village possessing the quality of extreme Wiltshireness. The locale is perfect, isolated in a valley under the Plain, with the Wansdyke and barrows as its shield, and all around the long, flat summit of the downs making a serene line along the horizon.

Long before the Domesday Survey the manor was a Royal gift to the See of Sarum, probably from a grant of the Crown of Wessex, and its name is, really, the Bishop of Sarum's Cannings, and there was once a bishop's palace there.

The church, rising majestically with its tall, and and small spire, is the focal point, the rest of the village clustering round with outlying farms and houses fringing the downs.

The earliest parts of the building date from 1150, and it is Bishop Jocelyn of Salisbury began its construction before he became a Cistercian monk in 1184. At that time, he was building on the foundations of an older church, fragments of which were discovered in the walls during restoration work in 1880.

Naturally, the Bishop built a Church worthy of his rich manor, and though time has made changes, it still retains the same lofty aspect, massive pillars and long chancel. An Elizabethan oak table replaces a stone altar in what is now the Ernle chapel in the south transept.

Sir John Ernle received permission to build pews in the chapel where he was buried in 1571 in a fine tomb emblazoned with his coat of arms and topped by a funeral helmet and wooden Saracen's head (as in the family arms).

The church contains a rare and unusual box-chair, somtimes called a "Meditation Chair", which now stands in the south transept. It is a high, box-like pew which seems to convey its own pessimism though this may be due to the gigantic, open hand — a left hand with palm outward, which was painted to fill the surface of the upper half of the taller side of the chair. Anyone sitting there would be able to see, on thumb, fingers palm and wrist, a succession of moral maxims, a dreadful chronicle of warning.

These maxims, in Latin. headed "Manus Meditacionis" — Hand of Meditation, are translated in a card attached to the pew. One reads:

"Thou shalt quickly be forgotten by thy friends. — Thy heir will seldom do anything for thee — He to whom thou leavest thy goods will seldom do anything for thee — Thy end is miserable."

There has been much conjecture about this strange pew, some believing it a pre-Reformation shriving pew, a confessional chair, and it is believed to be an unique example of the ancient "Garrel" stall usually fixed in the cloister of monastic buildings, used by the monks and clergy for private study and meditation.

Always a musical place (for James I and Queen Anne of Denmark were once entertained to a great musical entertainment there) it is fittting that the organ should have been provided by an endowment from a local boy who sailed with Captain Cook. Its bells are said to form a solid memorial to George Ferebe, one of its most celebrated Vicars,and a lasting tribute to his energy.

The church has a special feature which, until recently, was part of the traditional character of the village. The small, squat little steeple on the North east side of the spire is over two hundred years old, and its size was the object of much merriment from other villages. Old jokes like suggestions that it should be watered and manured to make it grow were legion, but the inhabitants soon learned to turn the amusment to their own advantage. The tall spire rises magnificently to a height of one hundred and thirty five feet, looking kindly down on its "baby brother".

THE WANSDYKE

Wansdyke is one of the finest linear earthworks in Britain, and though the two ends of this great ditch are nearly fifty miles apart, the work is not continuous.

An impressive section north of Devizes, at Morgan's Hill continues eastward over the downs to Savernake Forest with footpaths and bridle paths across the downs.

Its origins remain a mystery, though some claim it was built by the Saxons as a defence against the Danes, others that King Arthur erected it against the Saxons, though present evidence declares it was built in the 6th century AD.

WEATHER LORE

In a rural county such as Wiltshire, there is obviously much weather lore, for farmers and shepherds rely on the elements.

Many of the old supersitions regarding weather have survived and some prove true. Signs for rain are common. For instance, when geese congregate and honk; when toads are active; sheep rise early to graze; cats playing like kittens and spiders sitting at the entrance to their webs are just a few:

An old rhyme goes —

If ash comes out before the oak
We shall surely have a soak.
If the oak comes out before the ash,
We shall only have a splash.

Some older folk shake their heads and mutter darkly, "A green January (one lacking in ice and snow) makes a full churchyard."

Naturally, in a county of Moonrakers, the moon plays a real part in weather forecasting. Some say, a ring round the moon forecasts wet weather, and the closer the ring the further off the rain. A moon on its back would mean wet, stormy weather.

One old Wiltshire belief was that the first twelve days of any year will be a guide as to the weather for the whole year.

THE WEAVERS OF WILTSHIRE

The west of Wiltshire, with its rivers and streams, was particularly suitable for weaving over the centuries, and at one time, the county rivalled Yorkshire as a wool centre, many weavers coming from the Continent to work in the county.

Several towns were particularly noted for their weaving — Trowbridge, now the county administrative capital, still retains some of the old weavers' houses with their large, upstairs windows to let in the light for the looms.

Warminster and Westbury were thriving wool centres, though the former was well known for its great wheat market. At one time, it was said that three hundred sacks of wheat changed hands in a single morning.

Weaving towns and villages flourished — Steeple Ashton, originally named Staple Ashton; Bradford on Avon; Seend; Castle Combe, Corsham, which still retains a row of the Flemish Weavers' cottages; Melksham and Chippenham among them.

Unfortunately, the wool trade declined and the smell of cloth no longer permeates the clear air of these places, but memories linger.

WHITE HORSES

Wiltshire is famed for the white horses cut into its chalklands, and in the last war, these had to be covered in case they were recognised as landmarks.

Of these, the oldest is the Westbury White Horse. Measuring one hundred and eighty feet in length, it is one hundred and seven feet high, and the eye alone is twenty-five feet round. It was cut to commemorate Alfred's victory over the Danes, but the original outline was changed when it was restored in 1778.

Cherhill is said to be the "best" White Horse. This is one hundred and thirty feet in length, and was cut on the slopes above the village of Calne by Doctor Alsop. It is said that he stood a mile away and shouted instructions through a trumpet to the workers! This White Horse was cut in 1780 and can be seen for miles around.

Alton Barnes, White Horse, the youngest of these three, was the creation of Robert Pile who had it cut in 1812.

He hired a journeyman-painter, John Thorne, to do the work for £20. and the figure was mapped out, the men hired to cut the turf and no more was heard of Thorne who disappeared with the money!

WILTON

Once the county town of Wiltshire after which it was named, it was one of the oldest boroughs in England before local Government was reorganised, and lies on the southern border of the Plain on the confluence of the Rivers Nadder and Wylye.

In Saxon times it was very important, sharing with Malmesbury the earliest known coins in Wiltshire, but its mint closed in the reign of Henry II.

The Leprosy Queen is a ghost said to haunt a hospital of St Giles which was founded by Adelaide, second wife of Henry I, for lepers. She has been seen within living memory, perhaps keeping an eye on her foundation for the charity still exists in the form of almshouses at Pugglestone.

The parish church has a link with America. It was restored in 1844 by the American Ambassador in memory of an ancestor and has steps one hundred feet wide and a tower a hundred feet high, linked by a cloister. One rare monument from Wilton House, shows the arms of Philip and Mary which is an unusual piece of heraldry in a church window.

In these days, Wilton is still one of the most attractive towns in the county and is world known for the manufacture of its carpets. The craft of carpet weaving has been practised here for centuries, being granted a Royal Charter in 1659.

Once a flourishing market town, the Fair rights belonged to the Abbess of Wilton, to hold a fair on St Matthew's Day, and at the famous nineteenth century Sheep Fairs some forty thousand sheep changed hands in a day.

Wiltshire itself grew out of Wilton which was the administrative centre for part of Wessex.

WILTON HOUSE

Built on the site of a Saxon Abbey, Wilton houses one of England's most beautiful stately homes.

For over a hundred years it has been the seat of the Earls of Pembroke, and the present house was completed in 1653, following a fire in 1647, so all that remains of the original Tudor building is the centre part of the east front.

Of great historical and architectural interest it spans the sixteenth to the nineteenth centuries with ease — a place partly designed by Inigo Jones, it is also where Shakespeare once acted.

There is a famous collection of paintings, furniture and sculpture in the state rooms including the double and single cube rooms.

The twenty acres of grounds include lawns with giant Cedars of Lebanon, the oldest of which was planted in 1630, and they were among the first trees to be brought from Lebanon.

Wilton is lived in which adds to its charm. Among its delights are electric light switches designed in the form of the Herbert family coat of arms, and the treasures include — a lock of Queen Elizabeth I's hair, Napoleon's despatch box, a Roman Senator's chair and an Indian Mutiny Gun.

THE WILTSHIRE CONSTABULARY

Ever in the forefront of service, it is not surprising that the Wiltshire Constabularly was the first County Force to be raised, when, on the 28th November 1839, Captain Samuel Meredith was appointed the first Chief Constable.

A retired Naval Officer, he entered the Royal Navy on the 8th May 1808 as a Volunteer ending his service with the Coast Guard as an inspecting Commander.

Captain Meredith retired from the Police Force in in 1870 to be succeeded by another Naval Officer, Captain R. Sterne, who was wounded at the bombardment of Odessa and Sebastopol, and was on "special service" on the north-east coast of Ireland during the Fenian disturbances, and like his predecessor, was also in the Coast Guard.

Colonel Sir Hoel Llewellyn succeeded him in 1908 dying in office in April 1945, to be followed, in turn, by Colonel H. A. Golden who served from 1946 to 1963.

The present Chief Constable, Mr G. R. Glendinning, was also a Naval man and took up his appointment in 1963.

It is of note that in the one hundred and thirty-seven years since the formation of the Wiltshire Constabulary, there have only been five Chief Constables, three of whom have been Naval Officers.

WILTSHIRE MEAT PASTE

Ingredients:

I lb lean beef

1 tablespoon anchovy paste (or sauce)

½ teaspoon pepper

Salt (to taste)

½ grated nutmeg

Put all ingredients in a basin after mincing thoroughly. Steam for at least 2 hours. When cold it is suitable for spreading on home-made bread or dry toast.

THE WILTSHIRE REGIMENT

There may be larger counties than Wiltshire and older regiments that the Wiltshires, but no county in Britain can have more reason for pride in its regiment, nor men more cause for loyalty.

Spanning two centuries of distinguished service, remembered in 1956 at the Bicentenary celebrations, the regiment was first raised in 1756 at Torbay — the second battalion of the 4th Foot, many of the recruits coming from Wiltshire. In 1758, the battalion, now a separate entity, was renumbered as the 62nd Foot, receiving the title of "Wiltshire" in 1782.

In 1804, it raised its own second battalion which served with distinction throughout the Napoleonic Wars, at the end of which it was disbanded.

In 1824, the 99th Foot was raised at Glasgow and known as the Lanarkshire Regiment. Its association with HRH The Duke of Edinburgh in South Africa and at home led to the granting of the title, "The Duke of Edinburgh's," in 1874, a title it bears proudly to this day.

The 62nd and 99th Foot were joined in 1881 and became the Duke of Edinburgh's Wiltshire Regiment bearing this name until 1928.

Though the Regiment amalgamated with the Berkshire Regiment in 1959 to form the Duke of Edinburgh's Royal Regiment (Berkshire and Wiltshire) many old soldiers still recall with pride their days "in the Wiltshires".

In a regiment with such a long history, there is much to remember. It was in 1758, soon after its formation, that the 62nd was in action. Four companies sailed up the St Lawrence River, serving as Marines, and took part in the capture of Louisburg, so winning the Regiment's first Battle Honour. In memory of this service, *Rule Britannia* was played on certain occasions and watches were struck on a ship's bell.

Later, in troubled times, as today, other members of the Regiment served in Northern Ireland where, at Carrickfergus, they fought an outstanding action against a French force which had landed there. Though outnumbered and surrounded, they did not surrender, and, short of ammunition, they tore off their buttons to use as musket balls, and the delay they inflicted caused the eventual defeat of the enemy.

In the American War of Independence, the 62nd earned the nickname of "Springers" from General Burgoyne for their alertness and dash in action throughout the campaign.

As a fighting unit, the 62nd saw much action, serving in the West Indies and in Europe in the struggle against Napoleon, destroying his hopes in the Egyptian campaign of 1801. Service in Sicily formed the associations that led to the Maltese Cross Badge and gained more Battle Honours. They fought in America, but returned to Europe just too late to share in the glory of the French defeat at Waterloo.

Never long out of the fighting front, they served in India, and in 1845 at the famous and costly battle of Ferozeshah, they bore the brunt of the fighting and most of their officers were killed. The sergeants commanded the companies with such distinction that, to this day, colours are handed to a sergeant's keeping on the anniversary of the battle — a custom unique in the army.

The Crimea campaign brought them the honour "Sevastopol" and they were not in action again for half a century.

Meanwhile, the 99th, raised in 1824, were on an overseas tour that led them to India, China and South Africa. They gained their first honour in New Zealand and at the capture of Pekin in 1860, during the destruction of the great emperor's palace they collected treasure which they brought to Queen Victoria.

In the Zulu Wars they served with great courage, and early in their history, gained another nickname, "The Nines" which, tradition attributes to the expression "dressed up to the nines" being the origin of their smart turnout. Another nickname, coined by their dress, was that of "Shak" to represent the Shako worn in 1800 and called "Shak" by the men. The 99th were very smart in both drill and dress in 1857, and perhaps jealously by other troops, they were called "The Queen's Pets," or maybe it was because their officers wore more than the usual amount of gold lace on their uniforms. Again in Aldershot, they were called "Parkes' Pets" in 1870 after their Commanding General.

Perhaps the most famous of the nicknames, and the most appropriate, is that of "Moonrakers" from the county which bore the same name as the regiment, For years, Wiltshiremen have been known as Moonrakers and gradually this name became associated with the regiment.

Twenty-five years ago, the Wiltshires came back to England and, after marching through the streets of Devizes, went to their Regimental Depot where they remained for three months, the first and last time that a regular battalion was ever to do so.

Two members of the Wiltshire Regiment were awarded the highest award, the Victoria Cross. In the Great War, Captain R. F. J. Hayward, M,C,, of the 1st Battalion, was awarded his decoration for his bravery at Bapaume, where, in spite of the fact that he was buried, wounded in the head and rendered deaf, and had his arm shattered two days later, refused to leave his men.

In the Second World War, on 10th August 1944, Sergeant M. A. W. Rogers, fighting with the Regiment in Italy with a Carrier Platoon, drew upon himself the enemy's fire, and, one hundred yards ahead of his platoon, accounted for two of the enemy's posts, but was killed at point blank range.

It is interesting to note that the families of both these brave men donated their VCs to the Regimental Museum at Le Marchant Barracks, Devizes, where they may be seen on proud display.

The Museum (open five days a week) is rich in history, spanning many years and containing much of interest to soldier and civilian allke. There is a fine collection of uniforms, medals, regimental silver, weapons and the freedom scrolls for the Freedom of Borough of Devizes was also conferred on an old comrade and former Mayor of the Borough, Mr R. G. Maslen, who served in the first World War, for his work for the Borough as Alderman and Mayor over many years.

The Duke of Edinburgh's Royal Regiment was formed on the 9th of June 1959, when the 1st Battalion The Royal Berkshire Regiment (Princess Charlotte of Wales's) and the 1st Battalion The Wiltshire Regiment (Duke of Edinburgh's) were joined together. Field-Marshal His Royal Highness The Prince Philip,

Duke of Edinburgh, Colonel-in Chief The Wiltshire Regiment presented colours to his new Regiment, The Duke of Edinburgh's Royal Regiment (Berkshire and Wiltshire).

So, with the passing of the old Wiltshire Regiment and the formation of the new, history was made. No one can fail to regret the ending of two such regiments, but nothing can erase their memories, their proud histories, for service such as theirs can never be forgotten.

The Regimental Depot at Le Marchant Barracks, Devizes (named after Lieutenant-Colonel Sir Gaspard Le Marchant) no longer echoes to the sound of marching feet, bugles and military trappings, but the ghosts of long-dead soldiers walk the wide square, and the distant sound of a band catches the perceptive ear.

The Old Comrades Association, founded in 1910, fosters the old esprit de corps and does not forget former members in need or assistance — or their families.

The spirit and traditions of the fine regiment live on in the hearts of men, and each year, in June, the Old Comrades gather in Devizes for their Annual Dinner, followed next day by the Church Service and march back to barracks. Once again, old friendships are renewed, old battles refought and old comrades remembered. With such men and such loyalty it is certain that, though they have a new name, the Wiltshire will be a regiment of which its name county can be justly proud and the hearts of men will stir, the pulses quicken and the eyes gleam when the notes of the old march, "The Vly" sound across the square.

MICHAEL WISE

Appointed Master of the Choristers and Organist of the Cathedral in 1668, Michael Wise was a native of that city.

A clever musician, he found favour with Charles II and was appointed a gentleman of the Chapel Royal in the year 1675, and next became Almoner and Master of the Choristers of St Paul's Cathedral. However, he was suspended from his office, having, it was thought, offended the king by commencing the voluntary before the preacher had ended his sermon!

He returned to his native Salisbury, but was a man of a violent nature, often given to fierce quarrelling.

In August, 1687, after a row with his wife, he rushed shouting into the Cathedral Close. The Watch, thinking him a robber, stopped him and a scuffle ensued, in which Wise received a blow on the head which fractured his skull, and he lay dead before the Cathedral.

WISHFORD BREAD STONES

The cost of food is always of interest, but the village of Wishford has kept a close watch on the price of bread in particular.

For the last 175 years stone tablets in the churchyard wall at Wishford Magna, near Salisbury, have recorded the rising price of bread.

Most of the stones mark outstanding periods of historical change — the effect of the Industrial Revolution in the nineteenth century, the First and Second World Wars and the change to decimal currency.

There are now seven stones, the first dating from 1800 and the latest, added by a local builder, is dated 1971.

WITAN MEETING

The year 978 saw a strange and unusual happening at Calne.

All the chief Witan of England were gathered there for an important meeting held in a "specially prepared high house of timber, open on each side that no deceit should lurk in vaults, and covered above against the injury of the air."

The background to this meeting was that up to the year 900, most of the secular clergy in England were married, and, in many monastries no vow of celibacy was required and many monks took wives. The followers of St Benedict and observers of strict monastic life found this a great affront and made efforts for reform. Naturally, there was much opposition and for many years the Church was divided into two camps — the celibates and the Seculars. When Dunstan, who strongly upheld the purely monastic system, became Archbishop of Canterbury, he resolved to end the controversy by obtaining the consent of the Witan for his reforms.

A meeting was held at Winchester but, owing to the violence of both parties, nothing was settled and the meeting adjourned "amid scenes of great confusion."

Eventually, the adjourned meeting took place at Calne, probably because Edward, who was now King, was there, and had been crowned by Dunstan in spite of much opposition from those who supported Ethelred. There was much bitterness on both sides.

Bishop Beornhelm was the last speaker for the Seculars and spoke so movingly that Dunstan's only reply was that he himself was an old man whose only desire was to live in peace. "As for our cause," he said, "it is the cause of Heaven, and to God we leave the decision."

No sooner had he spoken, than, with a dreadful crash, the floor gave way and all save Dunstan were precipitated to the ground below. Scarcely one of those who fell escaped injury or death. Dunstan escaped as the throne on which he sat rested on a beam.

The regulars considered this tragic event a direct intervention from God on their behalf, and, this view also being taken by the people, they were able to carry out the reforms desired.

THE WITCH OF WINTERSLOW

In the eighteenth century, a man called Collins told how, as a boy in Winterslow in 1872, he remembered seeing Thomas Shears, son of "Liddie" Shears said to have been a witch. He used to haunt the neighbourhood of his mother's cottage.

Old Lydia or Liddie Shears was reputed to have been a witch and it was said that, if the local poachers did not take her some "snuff and baccy" there would be no hares for them to catch. If the snuff and baccy were given, old Liddie would go round the fields on moonlit nights with a flint and steel to strike sparks which caused the hares to sit up, and to be shot down by the poachers. This happened about 1816.

Liddie Shears' cottage was a lonely one and local people were said to have dread of her. Farmer Tanner, who lived a little distance away, kept a stud of greyhounds for coursing and passed her cottage often, always asking her where he would find the hares. And she would tell him. The hare was always there but was also always lost at the back of Liddie's cottage. The farmer could not understand it, so he asked advice of the Rector who advised him to make a bullet from a silver sixpence, shoot the hare when it came within sight of the cottage. This was done and the hare shot dead as it entered the garden. Afterwards, when Farmer Tanner called at the cottage, there was no sign of the hare, but Liddie Shears lay dead on the floor. Upon examination, the silver bullet was found to have caused her death.

THAT LOVELY WOODLAND

One of Wiltshire's most beautiful inheritances must surely be the unique stretch of woodland near Marlborough known as Savernake Forest. It is said there is nothing to compare with it in the whole of southern England, and it is certainly a lovely and magnificent place.

The only English forest which is the property of a subject, the succession of its hereditary wardens has never been broken over the centuries.

For over four thousand acres, wth a circumference of sixteen miles, the oak, ash and beech trees which predominate stretch across the countryside. These days, it is divided into avenues, and the one called Grand lives up to its name, a wide road, over three miles in length which stretches to Tottenham House, once the home of the wardens. There are, however, still tiny glades and unexplored paths where one may see the birds and animals which once roamed so freely.

As with most old places, the forest claims its share of ghosts. Many kings hunted there with their friends, and the glades are said to echo to the cry of the hunting horn and the champing of the horses. One of its most famous visitors, for he came to court one of its daughters, was Henry VIII whose wedding feast to Jane Seymour (the only wife to bear him a son) was celebrated at Wulfhall in the heart of the forest. Henry returned to the forest when a widower, and it is said, "his whole court came to Wulfhall to visit the late Queen's brother, and a great feast was held in the old barn from Saturday, August 9th 1599 until Tuesday, August 12th, two hundred people being entertained every day." Four years before his death, the King came again to Wulfhall, so his memories must have been happy ones, and if it is his ghost that rides in the glades, it would not be a sad apparition that crossed one's path.

The magnificence of some of the great oaks is, at all seasons, a wonder and delight. In spring, flushed with new greenery, and tiny shoots sprouting from all its branches, one of these oaks can show nature at its most promising. In high summer, with full leaf, it is a promise fulfilled, and in shades of autumn gold, and red, it is in full glory. Yet, somehow, in the bleak days of winter, with all its leaves gone the tree stark and bare, it seems, to me, to be at its most triumphant and inspiring.

WOODHENGE

The Neolithic site was said to be one of the first major discoveries by aerial photography in Britain.

Squadron Leader Insall flew over the site in 1925 and, following the report of his sightings, it was investigated by archaeologists.

The site is the first of a series of circular wooden structures of neolithic date to be found, and appears to be unique to Britain.

Once named, "A child's imitation of Stonehenge" it was felt to have been the wooden prototype for the stone structure.

It was a ceremonial site and the, apparently, sacrificial burial of an infant there, one of the few in England, was discovered when it was excavated.

WOOTTON BASSETT

After the Conquest, the Normans dispossessed many of the English and those who were not killed often went into exile, some remaining as nobodies. Often the English name of a property taken by the Normans merely acquired the addition of the Norman's own name and this still remains.

For example, Wootton — the woodland tun or farm — was well represented in Wiltshire and Wootton Bassett family. (Another Wiltshire Wootton is Wootton Rivers — the property of the Rivers family).

Today, one of the unusual features of this little town is the wide, main street where, in the middle, the pretty, half-timbered "Town Hall" is set up on stone pillars. The building, erected in 1700 by the first Earl of Rochester, was restored in 1889 and is now a library. Under the colonnade below, there are iron railings behind which lurk the old town stocks and ancient fire engine.

WORD ALE

Late into the nineteenth century a strange, secret religious ceremony was carried out at Wootton Bassett.

The annual ritual of "Word Ale", dating back centuries, took place at some time near the date of All Saints' Day in November. Tenants who lived on lands owned by the Lord of Wootton Bassett Manor were exempted from paying tithes if they took part in the rite.

The assembled company would sing hymns and drink a lot of ale!

They also offered prayers in memory of the twelfth century Cistercian monks who originally granted this exemption. The event was said to be recorded by cutting a notch in a hazel rod, a yard long, which was kept by the tenant whose turn it was to act as host the following year.

SIR CHRISTOPHER WREN

The village of East Knoyle lies in an attractive, woodland setting in one of the loveliest parts of the county and is particularly remembered as the birthplace of Sir Christopher Wren. His father was Rector here in 1632, and, though the great man's former home has long since disappeared, a stone marks his birthplace.

Everyone, the world over, knows and admires the great architect's work, particularly in restoring London after the Great Fire, and there are many Churches which bear testimony to his skill. His own memorial is in the most famous of all, St Paul's Cathedral.

Perhaps it is not so well known that he was keenly interested in anatomy, working with Charles II's own physician in coming down from Oxford. He began experimenting with techniques for blood transfusion, and, in 1656, carried out the first experiment of this kind by giving an intravenous infusion. This consisted of a suspension of wine, ale, opium, scammony and other substances which he injected into the veins of a dog and then studied the effects. Nine years later, this pioneer experiment bore fruit when one of his contemporaries, Dr. Richard Lowir, successfully transfused blood from one dog to another.

YEW TREES IN THE CHURCHYARD

Yew trees are often found in churchyards and are said to have formed part of a Pagan ritual.

A slow-growing and long-living tree, it is looked on as a symbol of immortality and particularly suitable for churchyards. (Evidently Field - Marshal Montgomery felt akin to them as he now lies buried beneath the shade of one).

The thick, close growth of the tree protected the church buildings against gales and storms, and it has been said a post of yew will outlast an iron post. It is poisonous to animals therefore farmers kept sheep and cattle away from it, as it guarded the church, and in the fifteenth and fourteenth centuries the longbow, made from the wood, was a successful weapon in warfare.

Branches of yew were often used to decorate churches and represent Palms on Palm Sunday in processions. In medieval times, Palm Sunday was often known as Yew Sunday.

Of the many yew trees gracing the churchyards of Wiltshire, one deserves special mention. It grows in the churchyard at Melksham — a fine specimen with its twenty limbs held up by some thirty props and shading a collection of table tombs.

ZEALS

This attractive village, with its thatched cottages and fine views, borders on Dorset and Somerset. It was the scene of excitement in 1651 when Charles II took refuge in Zeals House when on the run from Cromwell's men after the Battle of Worcester.

The house was the home of Colonel Hugh Grove who was executed at Exeter in 1655 for his part in the Royalist rising under Colonel Penruddock.

A SECRET PLACE

Set in the heart of Wiltshire, not far from my home, is for me a very special place.

A wild and lonely hill, with a fringe of trees clustered together for protection, makes a marvellous vantage point to view many miles of typical Wiltshire landscape. It is all here, the gentle slope of the green downs, undulating and rising in a broad sweep, the Wansdyke like an enormous basin dipping into eternity and the cluster of tiny cottages round a church in the far, far distance.

This place offers beauty in its seclusion, for the only sounds are the distant hum of farm tractors on the far edge of a huge field, and sweet birdsong fills the clean air. My small, sturdy Jack Russell dog and I think this our favourite place, where none disturbs our tranquillity, and I can laugh at his struggles to reach the top of the hill and bark defiance at the colony of rooks nesting and gossiping in the trees at the summit. For him, the area offers endless enjoyment and excitement, and I am sure he regards it, as I do, as his very own. One day, he will run in a frantic, useless chase across the newly-ploughed field, to halt in a lurching swerve if a bird, startled in its nest, rises up in protest in front of him. Another, he will race to an old, half-empty pond, puzzled by the sarsen stones lying there like sentinel sheep to be approached with caution.

Whenever I have been away from home, or feel troubled, this is the place to seek to find peace of mind. A walk in the clear air of this place where Time's hand has seemingly passed unheeding, is a wonderful restorative, and soon everything is back in perspective. The very timelessness of this land restores one's equilibrium and one's faith in life itself.

In the bleak days of winter, when the fields are bare, the trees a mere scratch of branches, one senses the promise of spring. That season, with the soft, warming air, filled with birdsong and freshness that is new, brings a hint of summer. Even on the hottest day when a relentless sun beats down, a gentle breeze trembles from the slope of the hill making it bearable and soon it is the turn of mellow autumn, when once more, the great fields lie fallow from ploughing and the sheep move from the pens to the sheltering farms,

At all times, my secret place brings me delight, and I seek no better.

Maybe, others know of it, but, thankfully, intruders are rare and the peace and solitude remain unviolated. Selfishly, I hope it can for ever be the place of my dreams and imaginings, my hopes and happiness.

THE END

Errata

Page 152. A Treasure at Place Farm.

Line 3 should read :

The old church dates back to AD 674 and Kipling's parents are buried in the churchyard where there is a

INDEX

INDEX

INDEX

INDEX

INDEX

INDEX